Baptism –

Sign and Seal of God's Grace

Baptism –

Sign and Seal of God's Grace

Brian A. Russell

Grace Publications

GRACE PUBLICATIONS TRUST
175 Tower Bridge Road
London SE1 2AH
England

Joint Managing Editors:
J.P. Arthur MA
D.P. Kingdon MA, BD

Distributed by
EVANGELICAL PRESS
Faverdale North Industrial Estate
Darlington
DL3 OPH
England

British Library Cataloguing in Publication Data available

ISBN 0 946462–62–3

Unless otherwise indicated the Scripture quotations are from the New King James Version of the Bible, copyrighted 1990 by Thomas Nelson Inc.

Printed and bound in Great Britain by
Cox & Wyman Ltd, Reading, Berkshire

To Muriel

My best friend, kindest critic, true yoke-fellow,
indefatigable typist and wife of my youth.

Contents

	Page
Foreword	9
Acknowledgements	11
Introduction	13
The history of baptism	16
The institution of baptism	28
The requirements for baptism	39
The necessity of baptism	47
The subjects of baptism (1)	54
The subjects of baptism (2)	67
The mode of baptism	80
The meaning of baptism	88
The purpose of baptism	94
The outcome of baptism	105
One baptism once	116

Foreword

Brian Russell is presently serving as the pastor of a Southern Baptist Convention church in the United States of America. He was born in South Africa where he pastored several churches with great distinction and ability. His preaching skill has often created a yearning amongst his hearers for something from his pen. 'Baptism – Sign and Seal of God's Grace' is the culmination of a first attempt to do this.

As the founder pastor of the Emmanuel Baptist Church, Florida Park, South Africa, Brian Russell preached and wrote about the importance of baptism. It was not his gospel, for he glories in nothing else, save in the cross of our Lord Jesus Christ. However, his concern for the authority of Christ, who instituted baptism and intended it to be a blessing to the Church, led him to produce a document for the assistance of those who need to clarify their thinking on the matter. When he was asked for permission to publish his work, he happily consented. We now have the pleasure of making available one of the best short treatises on baptism today. It is sufficiently brief to be read in one sitting, yet adequately comprehensive to deal with the usual problems posed by paedo-baptists.

Baptism has been referred to as the water that divides. The intention behind this publication is certainly not to add to that division. Its main purpose is to show that there is a clear case for believers' baptism by immersion, and that submission to this sacrament can only be to the believer's benefit.

It is hoped that the circulation of this book will add to the growing number of people who have come to a better understanding of our 'one Lord, one faith and one baptism' (Eph. 4:5).

Martin Holdt
Pastor, Emmanuel Baptist Church
1988

Acknowledgements

No one was more surprised than I to receive a gracious request from Pastor Martin Holdt in 1988 to publish my baptismal class lessons for use in the churches of the Baptist Union of South Africa.

I had served there as a pastor for 20 years and became very good friends with Martin, a kindred spirit in the Lord, in doctrine and in piety. I am deeply grateful to him and to the anonymous benefactor who financed the first publication under the direction of Emmanuel Baptist Church, Florida Park where Martin and I both had the joy and privilege of serving.

I would also like to thank Grace Publications of England for their encouragement and assistance to republish the book for a much wider readership. Their corrections and suggestions have much enhanced the overall presentation of the material contained therein.

There is nothing original which has been expressed, and I would be very remiss if I did not acknowledge my profound indebtedness to the many godly authors of different persuasions to whom I have referred and from whose teaching I have greatly benefited. If I have omitted to give due credit to some of them it is because in giving up two-thirds of my library in 1982 on moving to the United States to pastor a Southern Baptist Church in Virginia, I have been unable to trace or recall my sources of help. I humbly apologise to them.

My supreme thanks, of course, goes to the God and Father of my Lord and Saviour Jesus Christ who, 49 years ago drew me to himself in repentance and faith (notwithstanding my recalcitrance) and 'through the washing of regeneration and renewing of the Holy Spirit' (Titus 3:5) portrayed and pledged to me in believer's baptism by immersion his wondrous grace of salvation through Jesus Christ for undeserving, hell-bound sinners.

January 2000

Introduction

Baptism is one of two ordinances which the Lord Jesus Christ has commanded his church to observe in every land and in every age until he returns to consummate his kingdom on earth. In essence we may define it as a religious rite administered in the name of the triune God and requiring the immersion of a penitent and believing sinner in water as a sacred sign and seal of the grace of salvation he or she has received through union with Christ by faith.

It is a sad fact, however, that just a few generations after the death of the last apostle, baptism became the subject of controversy in the early church. For reasons given near the end of chapter one, differences of understanding began to appear among Christians regarding the mode of baptism, its meaning and who should receive it. These conflicting opinions have resulted in different denominations and some, in reaction to the division that has been caused, have turned their backs on baptism altogether and refuse to administer the ordinance at all. Such is the position taken by Quakers and the Salvation Army.

Of course, even when the apostles were alive the church had its differences of conviction, especially over the issue of whether circumcision was binding on Gentile converts or not. But baptism was not one of those issues on which the apostolic church was divided. In Ephesians 4:5 Paul says there is only 'one baptism' which means there is only one true mode (or right way) to carry out the practice, only one meaning as to its significance and only one category of people who can qualify to be baptized. The purpose of this book, therefore, is to help enquiring Christians to discover the oneness of baptism in the Scriptures.

But to be true to the biblical doctrine of baptism it is important for us to recognise and affirm that Christian baptism is both an 'ordinance' and a 'sacrament'. The word ordinance emphasises the duty of obeying Christ's command to be baptized. The word sacrament emphasises the purpose of baptism as a witness and pledge of God's grace and our response to it. Both words are needed to describe baptism.

Most Baptists and Pentecostalists shy away from the word sacrament and I can understand their apprehension, because it is used by some Christians in a sacerdotal sense (that is, as having supernatural power to save with or without personal faith). But in itself, the word sacrament is an innocent word for a sacred sign given as a solemn pledge. The Latin word *sacramentum* means 'oath'. It was the oath of allegiance which bound a Roman soldier to the officer enrolling him. But for a Christian it is not only a pledge of loyalty to God, it is also God's pledge of faithfulness to him or her to fulfil what he has promised them in the covenant of grace and salvation. This is how the Jews viewed circumcision (Rom. 4:11) under the old covenant. But in the New Testament baptism has replaced circumcision as 'the sign and seal of the righteousness of the faith' promised to Christians under the new covenant (Col. 2:11,12).

The word sacrament (meaning a sacred seal or pledge) is the only word I know that can adequately describe the binding obligation into which God and man enter in the covenant of grace. To surrender it to sacerdotalists is unnecessary and self-impoverishing. All Bible-believing Christians of whatever denomination can surely agree with the Westminster Confession of Faith's definition: 'Baptism is a sacrament of the New Testament, ordained by Jesus Christ, not only for the solemn admission of the party baptized into the visible church, but also to be unto him a sign and seal of the covenant of grace, of his ingrafting into Christ, of regeneration, of remission of sins, and of his giving up unto God through Jesus Christ, to walk in newness of life' (chapter XXV111).

Baptism is truly a many-splendoured thing, as we shall seek to show. It marks the beginning of a new life 'in Christ' (2 Cor. 5:17), the first great milestone a converted Christian passes on his or her pilgrimage to heaven. At baptism a Christian signs on for the Christian race. He or she enlists as a volunteer in the Lord's army and vows to be a faithful soldier and servant to the end of life. Not in their own strength, of course, but in the strength of the grace God pledges to them in his spoken and visible word (baptism).

When seen as such, baptism is a very solemn and important step in one's Christian life and should never be approached with anything less than sincere thoughtfulness to discover God's will revealed in his Word. May God in his mercy use the contents of this book to help you prepare for your baptism as carefully and prayerfully as possible. Or, if you have already been baptized as a believer, may you gain a clearer understanding of the meaning and purpose of baptism.

Chapter One
The History of Baptism

Before our Lord Jesus Christ instituted Christian baptism in the great commission he gave to the Church in Matthew 28:18-20, it was already being practised by others as the Gospels clearly indicate. It was not a totally new religious ceremony which he brought into being. He therefore did not have to explain what he was requiring from his disciples by ordaining this religious rite and why. Though he had explained to his disciples on the eve of his crucifixion the requirements and meaning of the ordinance of the Lord's Supper (Luke 22:14-22), he did not do so in the case of baptism a few weeks later at his ascension. He simply made permanent and obligatory a ceremony which was already in existence and being practised by his disciples on a limited basis (John 4:1-2).

So to understand Christian baptism we must begin by looking at the way it was practised and taught prior to the Christian era. And as we do so we shall see that as it developed in its meaning and significance, the actual way it was carried out always remained the same (with one exception: baptism was now to be 'in the name of the Father and of the Son and of the Holy Spirit'). To begin with, we shall need to examine –

The baptism of proselytes to Judaism

Proselyte baptism was probably pre-Christian although the documentary evidence for it only dates from AD 70. The Pharisees, we are told, 'traverse sea and land to make a single proselyte' (Matt. 23:15). A proselyte was a Gentile converted from paganism to Judaism. But before a proselyte could be received into the membership of God's people, three things took place. First, a sacrifice had to be offered. Second, if the person was a male, he had to be circumcised. And third, the candidate was then baptized before three witnesses or sponsors, after confessing his sin and his new faith in the God of Israel. The baptism was by immersion and it was self-administered. The candidate sat in a bath and baptized himself, 'washing away Gentile impurities'.

The language the rabbis used of the newly baptized proselyte is most instructive. They said he is 'like a new-born child', 'a new creation', that he has been 'raised for the Lord'. Accordingly, Gentiles who became Israelites in this way were described as 'born of water' and not of blood. Hence our Lord's use of the term in John 3:5, 'Except a man be born of water and of the Spirit, he cannot enter into the kingdom of God.' According to Jesus, it's not enough to be baptized in water to enter the kingdom of God; one must also be baptized in the Spirit and be born anew spiritually.

There is, therefore, a close link between proselyte baptism and Christian baptism, not only in the language used but also in the actions enjoined by both. And this correspondence cannot be by coincidence. 'The only possible conclusion is that the rites are related as parent to child' (J. Jeremias).

Despite this, it is important in view of the claim made by some that proselyte baptism provides an argument for baptising infants, to notice an important difference. Whilst the children of proselytes were also immersed, children born subsequently were not, on the ground that they were in the father's loins at the time of his baptism.

The baptism of John

John the Baptist had a unique commission to baptize. In John 1:33 he claims that God had sent him to 'baptize with water', and it is likely that he adapted proselyte baptism for the purpose of his peculiar mission. There was one big difference, however, and it was this: John commanded even those who were Jews by birth to submit to a rite which was devised exclusively for the benefit of Gentiles. In other words, John was treating his fellow Jews as sinners who needed to repent of their sins and be forgiven before they could enter the kingdom of God. Matthew 3:7-10 makes this very clear: 'But when he saw many of the Pharisees and Sadducees coming to his baptism, he said to them, "Brood of vipers! Who warned you to flee from the wrath to come? Therefore bear fruits worthy of repentance, and do not think to say to yourselves, 'We have Abraham as our father'. For I say to you that God is able to raise up children to Abraham from these stones. And even now the axe is laid to the root of the trees. Therefore every tree which does not bear good fruit is cut down and thrown into the fire."' As he saw it, what excluded men from the kingdom of God was not their physical descent (their Gentile birth), but their spiritual depravity (their inherent sinfulness).

John, therefore, preached the necessity of repentance for the remission of sins and offered baptism as a means by which they could publicly confess their sins and lay hold upon the hope of forgiveness from God. Actual participation in the act of baptism on the part of the candidate was itself an acted profession of repentance and John's administration of it to the penitent sinner was a pledge of divine remission. Mark 1:4-5 records that 'John came baptising in the wilderness and preaching a baptism of repentance for the remission of sins. Then all the land of Judea, and those from Jerusalem, went out to him and were all baptized by him in the Jordan River, confessing their sins'.

Here it is important to notice that John's baptism was anticipatory in that it looked forward to the one who would make good these promises. He, in contrast to John's ceremonial baptism with water, would baptize men with the Holy Spirit. Two passages make this clear. (1) Mark 1:7, 'And he preached, saying, "There comes one after me who is mightier than I, whose sandal strap I am not worthy to stoop down and loose;"' (2) John 1:29-33, 'The next day John saw Jesus coming toward him, and said, "Behold! The Lamb of God who takes away the sin of the world! This is he of whom I said, 'After me comes a man who is preferred before me, for he was before me.' I did not know him; but that he should be revealed to Israel, therefore I came baptising with water." And John bore witness, saying, "I saw the Spirit descending from heaven like a dove, and he remained upon him. I did not know him, but he who sent me to baptize with water said to me, 'Upon whom you see the Spirit descending, and remaining on him, this is he who baptizes with the Holy Spirit.'"

John's baptism was not only a symbol of promised cleansing, but also a symbol of anticipated spiritual quickening – of death to the old life of sin, and the beginning of a new life of holiness – a life characterised by the fruits of repentance (Luke 3:10-14).

Our Lord's own baptism

The head of the church who commanded his followers to be baptized, submitted to the rite himself and permitted his disciples to baptize (see John 3:22; 4:1-2). He made a two-day journey to the river Jordan to be baptized by John, who was naturally reluctant at first to do so. For if John's baptism was for penitent sinners who were confessing their need of cleansing from God, why should the sinless Son of God desire to be baptized? John was therefore hesitant to baptize Jesus: 'Then Jesus came from Galilee to John at the Jordan to be baptized by him. And John tried to prevent him, saying "I need to be baptized by you, and are you coming to Me?"' (Matt. 3:13-14). But when Jesus assured him that it was necessary 'to fulfil all righteousness', he consented. 'But Jesus answered and said to him, "Permit it to be so now, for thus it is fitting for us to fulfil all righteousness." Then he allowed him' (verse 15). What did our Lord mean by that phrase, 'to fulfil all righteousness'?

Well, to begin with, the word righteousness simply means doing what is right in the eyes of God. And since God required, through his prophet John, Jews to be baptized, the Son of God obediently fulfilled this divine requirement, even though in his sinless state it was not necessary for him to do so. He had no sins to confess and therefore nothing of which to repent. But he was baptized all the same because he came to be our representative, identifying himself with us sinners and taking our place. In other words, Jesus was baptized as an example of obedience for us. If this is what God requires of sinners, then as the representative of sinners he would fulfil the righteous requirements of God.

But there was something even more important about Christ's

baptism. It was not only an example of obedience for us to follow, it was also an outward picture of what would be required to make men righteous before God. For his baptism (literally, immersion) in water was a symbol of that greater baptism of suffering and death that would engulf his soul upon the cross. Luke 12:50 records him as saying, 'I have a baptism to be baptized with, and how distressed I am till it is accomplished!' Jesus was referring to his atoning death for sinners at Calvary. To Jesus Christ the waters of baptism were the waters of God's judgement upon the sin of all those he was going to save.

His coming up from the watery grave of baptism was also a picture of his resurrection and ascension by which the Father acknowledged and approved his work of redemption. That is what the voice from heaven was referring to when it said (verse 17), 'This is my beloved Son, in whom I am well pleased.'

And again, the descent of the Holy Spirit upon Jesus at his baptism in the form of a dove (verse 16), was not only God's promised anointing of power to fulfil his mission on earth (Luke 4:18 and Isa. 61:1-2), but also the witness and pledge that when his work was completed and he was glorified in heaven, the promised Spirit would be given to all for whom he died. Thus Jesus said to the crowds in John 7:37-38, '"If anyone thirsts, let him come to Me and drink. He who believes in Me, as the Scripture has said, out of his heart will flow rivers of living water." But this he spoke concerning the Spirit, whom those believing in Him would receive; for the Holy Spirit was not yet given, because Jesus was not yet glorified' (cf. John 1:32-33).

Here, then, our Lord's baptism in water points unmistakably to his death and resurrection as the source of the twin blessings of salvation – the forgiveness of sins and the gift of the Holy Spirit. And in the teaching of Jesus and his apostles this became the main and deeper meaning of baptism, namely, that baptism by immersion in water is a divine picture and pledge of a believer's union with Christ in the three great acts which have secured salvation: Jesus' death, burial and resurrection (Rom. 6:3-14).

Christian baptism

In the Old Testament circumcision was the 'sign' and 'seal' of the covenant which God made with the children of Israel through Abraham (Rom. 4:11). But hundreds of years later God's prophets predicted that this covenant would be replaced by a new covenant which would offer to God's people not only forgiveness for their sins, but also the power of the Holy Spirit to live a holy life. In Jeremiah 31:31-34 God gave his people this promise: 'Behold, the days are coming, says the LORD, when I will make a new covenant with the house of Israel and with the house of Judah – not according to the covenant that I made with their fathers in the day that I took them by the hand to lead them out of the land of Egypt, My covenant which they broke, though I was a husband to them, says the LORD. But this is the covenant that I will make with the house of Israel after those days, says the LORD: I will put My law in their minds, and write it on their hearts; and I will be their God and they shall be My people. No more shall every man teach his neighbour, and every man his brother, saying, "Know the LORD", for they all shall know Me, from the least of them to the greatest of them, says the LORD. For I will forgive their iniquity, and their sin I will remember no more.'

In Ezekiel 36: 24-27 God repeats this promise to his people

who were then in exile. 'I will … gather you out of all countries, and bring you into your own land. Then I will sprinkle clean water on you and you shall be clean; I will cleanse you from all your filthiness and from all your idols. I will give you a new heart and put a new spirit within you; I will take the heart of stone out of your flesh and give you a heart of flesh. I will put My Spirit within you and cause you to walk in My statutes, and you will keep my judgements and do them.' Forgiveness of sins (or cleansing) and the power of the Holy Spirit to keep God's commandments (or a new heart) are the twin blessings of salvation promised by God to his people under the new covenant.

It is therefore significant that on the eve of his crucifixion our Lord Jesus Christ inaugurated this new covenant at the last supper when he clearly and boldly took the cup of wine and said to his disciples, 'This cup is My blood of the new covenant, which is shed for many for the remission of sins' (Matt. 26:28). But it is not only the bread and the wine of the Lord's Supper that is a sign and a seal of the new covenant. So, too, is baptism by immersion in water. Thus in Matt. 28:18-20, just before his ascension to the Father's right hand, our Lord said to his disciples, 'All authority has been given to Me in heaven and on earth. Go therefore and make disciples of all the nations, baptizing them in the name of the Father and of the Son and of the Holy Spirit, teaching them to observe all things that I have commanded you; and lo, I am with you always, even to the end of the age.'

This was the moment when Christian baptism was officially instituted by our Lord and Saviour as the second ordinance or sacrament of the soon-to-be formed Christian church. First, like Jewish baptism and John's baptism, it involved the immersion of the candidate in water as an act of initiation into the company of God's people. It also demanded confession and repentance as the following passages show. Acts 2:38, 'Repent, and let every one of you be baptized in the name of Jesus Christ for the remission of sins.' But it did not stop there. It called for faith in Jesus as the Christ (or the Messiah), the Son of God and the Saviour of the world. Acts 8:12, 'But when they believed Philip as he preached the things concerning the kingdom of God and the name of Jesus Christ, both men and women were baptized.' (see also Acts 16:31-33).

Second, it was to be administered in the name of the triune God (Father, Son and Holy Spirit), something altogether new and foreign to Jewish thought. And then, thirdly, it was to be seen not as a pledge of the future blessings of forgiveness and the baptism of the Spirit as *future* blessings (as was the case with John's baptism), but of blessings *presently* available. For the one who was to make good the promises of John's baptism was Jesus Christ and he had come. By his death and resurrection he has procured as a present possession for all believers these blessings of the new covenant. Thus on the day of Pentecost, Peter could say to the multitude who were cut to the heart by his sermon and wanted to know what they must do: 'Repent, and let every one of you be baptized in the name of Jesus Christ for the remission of sins; and you shall receive the gift of the Holy Spirit' (Acts 2:38).

The emergence of infant baptism

The practice of believers' baptism by immersion as we have traced it, was perpetuated by the apostles and the early church. This can be substantiated by the apostolic writings themselves, the ruins of ancient baptisteries, and from the fact that post-apostolic writings show that believers' baptism was widely practised till the end of the fourth century. We shall give more proof of this in chapter 3 when we consider the 'subjects of baptism'.

Suffice it now to say that infant baptism only began to appear when the belief became widespread that baptism magically conveyed salvation. Superstitiously people began to believe that baptism by itself washed away a person's sin. And the logical conclusion of this belief was that the sooner a person was baptized, the safer it was for him. Thus infants were baptized as soon as possible after birth to ensure the removal of original sin; and all babies who died without being thus baptized were regarded as lost and condemned to hell. This view is still taught in many parts of Christendom, and is a major factor behind the concern of many parents to have their babies christened.

So from as early as AD 200 infant baptism began to assert itself, and once the meaning of baptism was lost, the mode itself became unimportant and was gradually changed for convenience sake. It should, however, be noted that immersion (of infants) has been retained by the Orthodox churches of the East and elsewhere to this day. The first recorded case of affusion (pouring) was that of a man called Novatian who lived about AD 250. Due to illness he could not leave his bed and so he was baptized by the pouring of water over his head. By about the fourth century affusion became the accepted method, but was gradually replaced by sprinkling which was less inconvenient and easier to administer to infants and the dying who, it was felt, had to be baptized for the forgiveness of their sins.

The recovery of believers' baptism by immersion

With the Reformation and the rediscovery of the biblical principle of salvation by faith in Christ alone, many who joined Luther and Zwingli in their revolt against the church of Rome were forced to reconsider the question of baptism. They discovered that the New Testament says nothing about infant baptism and was administered only to believers on profession of their faith in Christ. These people were dubbed Anabaptists (re-baptizers) because they baptized those who had already been baptized as infants. But the Anabaptists did not see their new baptism as a re-baptism, for they did not accept that infants were validly baptized. The first baptismal service of believers in the Reformation era was held in Zurich on 25th January, 1525, when Konrad Grebel baptized a former monk by the name of George Blaurock, who followed by baptising fifteen others.

Here was a parting of the ways. From this time on until the present day the question of believers' baptism in place of infant baptism has not ceased to be a matter of serious controversy in the Christian church. At the beginning many Anabaptists were either imprisoned, banished or martyred for their obedience to the Word of God. In January, 1527 Felix Manz was drowned in the River Limmat for practising believers' baptism. To the authorities it seemed poetic justice. Zwingli's comment was, 'Let him who talks about going under (the water) go under!' Ulrich Zwingli, the leader of the Reformation movement in Zurich, became a stormy upholder of infant baptism.

It was a sad day! Protestant had killed Protestant for the crime of obeying God's Word as he understood it. And to make matters worse, the Reformers knew that baptism for believers only by immersion was what the Bible taught. Zwingli, for example, had given baptism much thought. 'Nothing grieves me more than at present I must baptize children, for I know it ought not to be done ... but if I were to stop the practice of Infant Baptism, I would lose my office.' And again, 'I leave baptism untouched. I call it neither right nor wrong. If we were to baptize as Christ instituted it, then we would not baptize any person until he reached the years of discretion, for I find Infant Baptism nowhere written or practised. But we must practise it now so as not to offend our fellow men ... It is better not to preach (adult baptism) until the world is ready to receive it.'

Fortunately, there were men in the church ready to practise it. And the Anabaptist movement spread rapidly throughout Switzerland and into Europe. Robbed by death of their best leaders, some Anabaptists followed fanatics. But under the providence of God there emerged from the movement the various free churches which still practise the New Testament doctrine of believers' baptism – the Mennonites, the Baptists, the Christian Brethren and the Pentecostalists.

Chapter Two
The Institution of Baptism

Jesus Christ's commission (or missionary manifesto) is recorded in all four Gospels though it is expressed in different ways and given on different occasions (see Matt. 28:18-20; Mark 16:15-16; Luke 24:48-49 and John 20:21-23). In each case an aspect of the truth which the Church is commissioned to preach is stated; the responsibility of the Church concerning that aspect is declared; and the power in which the church is to discharge her responsibility is revealed. The fullest expression of our Lord's great commission was the last one given in Galilee and recorded in Matthew 28:18-20 in which he also officially instituted Christian baptism as the initiatory rite into the membership of his people or church.

We are not told who was present when Jesus uttered this version of his missionary manifesto, but it seems probable that it was the group of more than five hundred that Paul mentions in 1 Corinthians 15:6. There were obviously some there who had not yet seen the risen Christ and were a little doubtful as to whether or not he would appear. 'But when they saw him, they worshipped him' (verse17). And as they were all worshipping him, he uttered these majestic words, 'All authority has been given to Me in heaven and earth. Go therefore and make disciples of all the nations, baptising them in the name of the Father and of the Son and of the Holy Spirit, teaching them to observe all things that I have commanded you; and lo, I am with you always, even to the end of the age' (verses 18-20).

Although, as we have seen, baptism was practised before by the Jews and by John the Baptist and by the disciples of Jesus, there are some new features in our Lord's institution of the ordinance which make it different in some ways from its previous forms. In the first place –

Christian baptism rests upon the universal sovereignty of Christ

'All authority has been given to Me in heaven and on earth,' said Jesus (verse 18). Standing on the resurrection side of his grave, Jesus declares his universal sovereignty in the simplest language. His claim admits of no qualification or limitation. His lordship, given by divine right, extends over the whole universe. The word translated here as authority does not suggest power in the sense of energy or might, but rather the power of choice (the right to choose); the power of enforcement (the right to insist upon obedience); and the power of government (the right to pass sentence on what is done). And it's on the basis of this universal authority that Jesus commissions his disciples to carry the gospel far beyond the confines of Palestine to every country in the world, making disciples of those who believe, baptising them, and then instructing them in the implications of the Christian life as taught by himself.

Christian baptism, therefore, rests upon a divine command that is absolutely binding upon everyone in every land and in every age until our Lord comes again. That is important, because some would like to limit baptism to the East or the so-called Third World. Finding public immersion in water a little embarrassing, they argue that whilst it may be alright for uncivilised people, it is out of place in the sophisticated Western world.

The answer to this objection, however, is that the command to baptize stands or falls with our Lord's two other commands to evangelise the unbeliever and to instruct the believer. And since Christian evangelism and Christian teaching are intended for every country, it follows logically that Christian baptism is as well.

Others argue that Christian baptism was a temporary rite to be practised only in the early church. It was not meant for all time. But we note again that our Lord Jesus commands that baptism should accompany evangelism until he returns in glory. The charge clearly implies that his threefold commission to evangelise, baptize and teach applies in its entirety until the end of time, for it closes with the promise, 'And lo, I am with you always, even to the end of the age' (verse 20).

Seeing, then, that the command to be baptized rests upon the absolute universal lordship of Jesus Christ and is to be observed by the Christian Church until he comes again, our personal obedience to this command is not an option but a supreme obligation. It is not for us to dispute and argue over our Lord's commandments but to obey them. Baptism, then, is not subject to our own particular inclinations or opinions. It is as mandatory and necessary as the Lord's Supper is.

Christian baptism marks the commencement of Christian discipleship

To understand and appreciate this fully, it is important to see that the Greek word *mathetēuō* ('make disciples') is the main verb and the central command of our Lord's great commission. The root meaning of the term is not simply to make men learners, but followers of Christ and his teaching. The Church is not just to instruct the minds of men in the truth, but to get men to believe the truth and to act upon it. In John 8:31 Jesus says, 'If you abide in My word, then you are truly My disciples.' We are not Christ's disciples if we do not abide by his teaching and submit to his Lordship.

Now sandwiched between the charge to make disciples of all the nations and to teach the new converts and followers of Jesus, is the command to baptize them. Baptism is intended to follow evangelism and to come before fuller instruction in the Christian faith. Our Lord's words make it clear that instruction in the faith is a continuous process which goes on long after baptism. This was certainly the pattern in the early church: the baptized converts, says Luke, 'continued steadfastly in the apostles' doctrine' (Acts 2:41-42).

We are, therefore, not baptized to testify that we are perfectly instructed Christians. We are not to wait until we are masters of the Bible from Genesis to Revelation before we submit to baptism. Instruction in the apostles' doctrine is something that is to continue right through the years of our Christian discipleship. We are to go on learning the mind of Christ more perfectly every day.

We are to be baptized, however, at the very commencement of our Christian discipleship. This witnesses to the fact that we have turned from our sin in repentance and have received Jesus Christ by faith as our Saviour and Lord. Baptism is intended to mark the beginning of our Christian life. So the sooner after our conversion we are baptized, the nearer we shall be to the New Testament pattern.

This does not mean, of course, that baptism requires no

instruction. It most certainly does. It requires instruction in God's way of salvation – the instruction which Sunday after Sunday is the heart of all true gospel preaching. The truths essential to our salvation must be experienced and intelligently grasped before baptism. The people of the nations are not to be baptized indiscriminately. Only those who are persuaded to give up their worship of false gods and to become the disciples and followers of Jesus Christ are to be baptized. Or, if you like, Christian baptism is a confession of faith made by those who have become disciples. It is not to be administered in hope that those who receive it may one day become disciples.

Christian baptism proclaims the greatness of our salvation

In his institution of Christian baptism in Matthew 28, our Lord draws attention to the verbal declaration made at baptism. The believer or disciple is to be baptized 'into the name of the Father and of the Son and of the Holy Spirit'. These moving, august words testify to the greatness of our salvation, and they do so in three ways.

(1) The source of our salvation

Our salvation is derived from the joint source of the blessed Trinity: it is from Father, Son and Holy Spirit. Every baptized believer should entertain this majestic view of his redemption. Ours is no small redemption! The Scriptures speak of it as 'so great a salvation' and an 'eternal salvation' (Heb. 2:3; 5:9). These are the only adjectives which we can use of the salvation which requires the work of all three Persons of the Trinity.

For our salvation flows from the decree and plan of God

the Father. It did not originate on earth, but in heaven. It did not begin in time at Bethlehem and the manger, but in eternity at the throne of God. Long before the creation of the world, God the Father knew that man would fall into sin and in his great love and mercy he arranged a way for sinners to be saved. That is why Peter insists that although the Jews (and Romans) put Christ to death, his crucifixion had been determined long before in eternity past: 'This Jesus, delivered up by the predetermined plan and foreknowledge of God, you crucified and killed' (Acts 2:23). Paul stresses the same thought in Ephesians 1:3-5 when he says, 'Blessed be the God and Father of our Lord Jesus Christ, who ... chose us in Him (Christ) before the foundation of the world ... in love, having predestined us to adoption as sons by Jesus Christ to Himself, according to the good pleasure of His will.' Without this predetermined planning on the part of God the Father, our salvation could not, and would not, have occurred.

What great love motivated this arrangement by the Father! He surely had to love lost, helpless sinners very much to give up the ineffable fellowship he enjoyed with his beloved Son throughout eternity. No wonder Paul says in Romans 5:8, 'God demonstrates His own love for us, in that while we were still sinners, Christ died for us.' And John 3:16 declares that 'God so loved the world that He gave His only begotten Son, that whoever believes in Him should not perish but have everlasting life.' We shall never know the full extent of the Father's love for lost sinners that moved him to give his Son as a ransom for our sins. We can only stand amazed before it, in wonder lost.

Then again, our salvation was accomplished by God the Son, for it required the sacrifice of an infinite being to pay the ransom necessary to redeem us from our sins. He who was

God, by whose word the world was created and continues to be sustained, had to strip himself of untold glory to become the babe of Bethlehem and the carpenter of Nazareth and to have no place whereon to lay his head.

But this mighty stoop of selfless love was as nothing in comparison with his sacrifice at Calvary's cross. For he whom angels worshipped gave his head to be crowned with thorns, his face to be spat upon, his hands and feet to be pierced with nails and his side to be thrust through with a Roman spear. But infinitely worse than that, the holy Son of God had to be separated from the Father, to be forsaken by him whose delight he had been throughout all ages, that he might become sin for us and bear its dreadful curse. To achieve the remission of our sins and our acceptance before a holy God, Jesus had to die the death of the cross, the death of eternal judgement, the death of God's inexorable wrath against sin, yours and mine. Our redemption was accomplished by the shed blood of the Son of God. Let us never forget that. And after he had paid the penalty of our sin by his atoning death, he rose again as 'the author of eternal salvation' (Heb. 5:9).

But the great plan of salvation arranged by the Father did not stop there. For the redemption accomplished at infinite cost by the Son of God had to be applied to us by God the Spirit. Without the ministry of the Third Person of the Holy Trinity we would still be complete strangers to God's salvation. For when our Lord ascended to heaven, he sent the Holy Spirit to 'convict the world of sin, and of righteousness, and of judgement' (John 16:8). It is God the Holy Spirit, and no mere human preacher, who preaches the gospel in our hearts, so that we see and believe that the Lord Jesus Christ has taken away the penalty of our sins and is able to deliver us daily from sin's power.

The Holy Spirit alone gives us 'deciding grace' and enables us to commit ourselves to Christ, for none of us believes in his own strength. 'No one can come to me', said Jesus, 'unless the Father who has sent me draws him' (John 6:44). And it is by the Holy Spirit that the Father draws us to the Lord Jesus Christ in repentance and faith. When we open the door for Christ to come into our needy, sinful lives, the hand that nerves ours to draw back the bolt is the Holy Spirit's; and when our Lord comes into our lives to dwell, again the one who imparts Christ to us is the Holy Spirit. All the benefits of our salvation by repentance and regeneration are made ours by the Holy Spirit. It is his office to unite us with the Saviour.

So, you see, the invoking of the name of the Trinity over the believer's head in baptism testifies to the greatness of his redemption in its origin in the triune God. It is to acknowledge the Father as having predestined it, the Son as having purchased it and the Holy Spirit as having applied it. But these solemn, splendid words of the baptismal confession testify not only to the source of our 'so great salvation,' but also to –

(2) The surrender it involves

The expression 'in the name of' proclaims the surrender of the believer to the triune God that faith implies. Notice, it is not in the names of, but in the 'name of'; for the Father and the Son and the Holy Spirit have one name: the name of God. And Christian discipleship is the transfer of the ownership of our life to that one God who consists of three persons co-equal, co-eternal and indivisible. When a property is in somebody's name it is his legal possession. A change of name carries with it a change of ownership. So when a property is sold the title deeds are automatically changed and the new owner's name is written into them.

By the same token, the baptismal confession 'in the name of the Father and of the Son and of the Holy Spirit' testifies to the fact that becoming a Christian involves a change of ownership. We willingly renounce all claim to our lives and make ourselves over to God, so that God the Father, the Son and the Holy Spirit have sole command over our life (see 1 Cor. 6:19-20).

Moreover, this surrender happens gladly, especially when we appreciate the wondrous news that the Father, to deliver us from futility and slavery in this world and eternal punishment in the world to come, gave his beloved Son to redeem us by his precious blood, and the Holy Spirit to indwell us and to apply all the benefits of redemption to our lives. When we think upon God's amazing, incomprehensible love towards us, what can we do but sink reverently to our knees and vow solemnly that 'love so amazing, so divine, demands my soul, my life, my all'?

To believe, then, is not to hand over our life to God as a 'going concern.' Far from it. When the Holy Spirit convicts us of sin, he shows us that we are morally bankrupt and must therefore go into 'liquidation'. And the wonder of the gospel of God's grace is that he takes us over when we have nothing to our name but impossible debts. No wonder Jonathan Edwards, when he came to this realisation, wrote these words in his journal: 'I have this day been before God and have given myself (all that I am and have) to God; so that I am in no respect my own. I can challenge no right in myself: in this understanding, this will, these affections. Neither have I the right to this body of any of its members; no right to this tongue, these hands, these feet, these eyes, these ears. I have given myself clean away.' This surrender is of the essence of faith and must be confessed in our baptism. But there is still more to the blessed words of the baptismal confession. They proclaim the comforting truth of –

(3) The security that is pledged in our salvation

For what God takes over, he cares for. When a happy father registers his new-born child in his own name, he assumes the responsibility of taking good care of that infant. Within his means his child shall not want for any good thing. In like manner, when we repent of our sin and believe the gospel, God puts his name on our foreheads (Rev. 22:4). And by this act, God makes all our needs, both in this life and the next, his sole responsibility. How secure Christians are with such a name written over them! How comforting to know that the Father, the Son and the Holy Spirit are all engaged to guide and bring us at last to glory! To be the Father's child, the Son's bride, the Spirit's temple! We are not left alone to battle against the world, the flesh and the devil. We do not have to make ends meet out of our own poverty. We have all God's resources at our disposal. What God says to us in the hour of our believing, he instructs his ministers to publicly reaffirm to us in the hour of our baptism: 'Son, all that I have is yours' (Luke 15:31). How incredibly rich we are with the name of the Trinity upon us. Rejoice, believer, in your everlasting security!

Christian baptism issues in a life of further instruction and obedience

The church's mission is not simply to make disciples, but to teach those who have been baptized. A disciple is by definition a learner and a follower. Our Lord, therefore, in the institution of Christian baptism, ties his command to baptize the new disciples to the command (verse 20), 'teaching them to observe all things that I have commanded you'. God's word is like milk to a new-born Christian who needs to feed upon it constantly. The church, if it is a true church, will faithfully give Christ's teaching to all the disciples who make up its membership. The disciples who have been baptized into the church, on the other hand, will earnestly desire such teaching.

Good teaching, however, is not enough. The church's job is not only to instruct the new disciple's mind, but to exhort and to encourage him in the way he should 'observe' or obey Christ's teaching. In this, the letters of the apostles in the New Testament are perfect models: they begin with doctrine and conclude with duty. Christian baptism according to Matthew 28:20 must issue in the lifelong task of learning and obeying 'the whole counsel of God' (Acts 20:27).

Christian baptism prevails because of Christ's continual presence

The last words of verse twenty reveal the dynamic behind Christian baptism which will ensure its continuance throughout this age: 'and lo, I am with you always, even to the end of the age'. It is impossible to carry out the great commission prevailingly save in living fellowship with the risen Christ himself. We may preach the need for people to become disciples and be baptized, but our preaching will lack converting power unless the truth is proclaimed in living, personal fellowship with Jesus, who by his resurrection, turned seeming defeat into absolute victory. There can be no fear of failure if, as he has promised, the Son of God is with us 'all the days'.

Chapter Three
The Requirements for Baptism

When our Lord instituted baptism as an ordinance binding upon his church till the end of time, he made it perfectly clear that only those who had become his disciples were to be baptized. The word disciple means a learner and follower of Jesus Christ. In Acts 11:26 we read that 'the disciples were first called Christians in Antioch.' The question that we now need to face and answer is this: how does a person become a Christian or a disciple of Christ? If this is the condition for being baptized, what must people do to become what Christians are elsewhere called 'believers' (Acts 5:14) or 'followers' (1 Thess. 1:6)?

The whole of the New Testament is God's answer to that question, but we can surely do no better than to go to the first Christian sermon which was preached by Peter on the day of Pentecost and recorded for us in Acts 2. In fulfilment of his promise, our Lord poured out the gift of the Holy Spirit upon his church in Jerusalem on this special day, and as a result all the disciples were 'filled with the Holy Spirit and began to speak in other tongues (in foreign languages they had not learned) … the wonderful works of God' (verses 4 and 11). And when Jews who had come from other countries to observe the feast of Pentecost heard the disciples speaking in their own home language, 'they were all amazed and perplexed, saying to one another, "Whatever could this mean?"' (verse 12).

Well, this gave Peter a wonderful opportunity to preach the gospel to the crowd who had gathered to witness this amazing spectacle. And in his sermon he charged his hearers with wickedly crucifying Jesus of Nazareth whom God then raised up to sit at his right hand, where 'having received from the Father the promise of the Holy Spirit, he poured out this which you now see and hear' (verse 33). Their reaction to Peter's charge was dramatic: 'Now when they heard this, they were cut to the heart, and said to Peter and the rest of the apostles, "Men and brethren, what shall we do?" Then Peter said to them, "Repent, and let every one of you be baptized in the name of Jesus Christ for the remission of sins; and you shall receive the gift of the Holy Spirit"' (verses 37-38). Here the apostle Peter is insisting that his hearers must first repent before they can be baptized.

Repentance

Repentance is not a word that is often used in modern English. Most people today seem to confuse it with simply feeling remorseful about some failure in one's life – a feeling bad about something I have said or done. And, of course, it will be accompanied by deep feelings of guilt and unworthiness, but at root repentance is not remorse. For repentance is more than just a feeling; it is a concrete action. The word repent literally means 'to turn round or to change your mind.' It is something we have to do, and that is why it is expressed in the imperative. When Zacchaeus, a dishonest tax collector, encountered Jesus Christ, he repented of his sin, saying, 'Look, Lord, I give half of my goods to the poor; and if I have taken anything from anyone by false accusation, I restore fourfold.' And Jesus said to him, 'Today salvation has come to this house.' (Luke 19:8-9). Repentance is a change of mind which leads to an immediate change of life.

But how does this change of mind and life come about? Well, as you can see from Acts 2, it comes about by the preaching of the gospel. In his sermon, Peter confronted the people with the truth about Jesus Christ, as well as the truth about themselves. He tells them the truth about Christ's life: that his claims were attested 'by the miracles, wonders and signs which God did through him in your midst' (verse 22). Christ's death, he says, was no accident because he was 'delivered by the determined purpose and foreknowledge of God' to be crucified by 'lawless hands' (verse 23). 'Whom', Peter goes on, 'God raised up, having loosed the pains of death, because it was not possible that he should be held by it.'

The people had rejected Jesus as the Son of David and the promised Messiah, but God raised him from the dead to vindicate him. They despised him, but God exalted him to his right hand to wait 'till I make your enemies Your footstool' (verse 35). On these grounds, 'God now commands all men everywhere to repent, because He has appointed a day on which He will judge the world in righteousness by the Man whom he has ordained. He has given assurance of this to all by raising Him from the dead' (Acts 17:30-31).

Now in confronting his hearers with the truth about Jesus Christ, Peter was also confronting them with the truth about themselves. For the gospel is not simply the presentation of something that took place on a cross outside the walls of Jerusalem. It is also a declaration that because of their rejection of Christ, all men are under judgement.

True, some of the visitors at the feast of Pentecost had not rejected him as the crowds in Jerusalem on Good Friday rejected him. But rejection of Christ does not have to be solely in terms of blatant blasphemy or atheism, for rejection of Christ takes place when a man simply fails to respond to God's offer of mercy. When the gospel is preached and a man simply ignores it or puts off responding to it to some more convenient season, whether he is prepared to admit it or not, he is rejecting Christ as really as did those men who said, 'We will not have this man to reign over us' (Luke19:14) and 'Away with this Man … crucify him, crucify him!' (Luke 23:18,21). This being the plight of his hearers, Peter 'exhorted them, saying, "Be saved from this perverse generation"' (verse 40).

Confronted with the truth Peter's hearers, through the working of God's Spirit, became convicted by the truth. 'Now when they heard this, they were cut to the heart' (verse 37). This is the second step towards repentance. When a man can listen to the gospel and not become convicted, he is in a sorry condition. His conscience is unawakened and insensitive. But when a man becomes deeply concerned about his sin, it is a most healthy condition in which to be! The Holy Spirit is convicting him of sin, because he does not believe in Christ; and of righteousness, because his trust is in himself and his own righteousness; and of judgement, because he is following the devil who has already been sentenced to everlasting punishment in hell (John 16:8-11).

This is not a pleasant experience, but rather a very painful one. Many psychologists may dismiss guilt feelings as morbid and harmful, but guilt is not just some kind of personal hang-up. It is something real, something objective, that stands between my Maker and me. The God who rules this universe is not some impersonal energy; he is a moral being, he is a holy judge.

When we do wrong, we *offend* him. We are not just

transgressing some man-made social convention – we are offending God. So it isn't enough to be angry with ourselves, for whatever reason. We have to face up to the fact that *God* is angry. It is not enough to be sorry for ourselves; we have to face the fact that it is God supremely that we have injured. We can only really begin to deal with guilt when we understand this. Then my mind is no longer absorbed by thoughts of how my sin affects me, or even how my sin affects other people. I begin to feel burdened now about how my sin affects *God*. I am not my own judge and neither are they. I stand accountable before God's bar of justice.

Peter's hearers acknowledged this. 'Now when they heard this, they were cut to the heart' (verse 37). It was as if a sword or knife went right through them. Their consciences were stirred and they were in great agony of soul. This is reflected in the question which then burst forth from them, 'Men and brethren, what shall we do?' The truth of the gospel which they had heard enlightened their minds, awakened their consciences and now challenged their hearts. Their cry was full of anxious enquiry. To whom could they turn? Where could they find peace for their troubled souls? Peter pointed them to Jesus Christ. 'Repent, and let every one of you be baptized in the name of Jesus Christ for the remission of sins; and you shall receive the gift of the Holy Spirit' (verse 38).

Now implicit in Peter's answer is another requirement for baptism, namely faith which is publicly expressed in baptism. It is most important to see how the apostle at this point unites repentance and baptism. He doesn't say, 'Repent and be saved, and some time later we can discuss baptism.' Rather, he puts the two together, because he is thinking of baptism as something more than just an outward ceremony involving water. Baptism here in Acts 2:38 stands for faith and all that it involves.

Faith

To grasp the connection between baptism and faith here, we need to compare Peter's reply with other statements made elsewhere in the New Testament. When our Lord began preaching, his first recorded words were, 'The time is fulfilled, and the kingdom of God is at hand. Repent and believe in the gospel' (Mark 1:15).

In Acts 16:31, when the Philippian jailer cried out in anguish of soul, 'What must I do to be saved?' the apostle Paul replied, 'Believe on the Lord Jesus Christ, and you will be saved, you and your household ... And immediately he and all his family were baptized.' Now he was a pagan and therefore did not know about needing to be baptized. So if he was baptized at once, it is quite clear that Paul and Silas in their preaching of the gospel, presented not only the call to faith, but the call to baptism as well.

In Acts 20:21 Paul says to the Ephesian elders, 'I kept back nothing that was helpful, but proclaimed it to you ... testifying to Jews and also to Greeks, repentance toward God and faith toward our Lord Jesus Christ.' This was Paul's message: repentance and faith; turn from your sins and believe on the Lord Jesus Christ.

Now the implication is surely this. If in reply to the question, 'What are we to do?' Peter says, 'Repent and be baptized,' and the gospel call is constantly, 'Repent and believe,' then quite clearly the call to be baptized is virtually interchangeable with the call to believe, because baptism was the opportunity for these enquirers to declare openly and publicly before men that they were believing, that they were trusting in Christ. So because the outward sign speaks so clearly and so vividly of faith, Peter on this occasion can use it instead of speaking of believing. 'Repent and be baptized' is exactly the same as saying, 'Repent and believe.'

In Peter's sermon there are two things about faith that we need to understand. The first is this: faith is personal trust in Christ for the remission of sins and the gift of the Holy Spirit. That is what Peter means when he says, 'and let every one of you be baptized in the name of Jesus Christ for the remission of sins; and you shall receive the gift of the Holy Spirit.' For to be baptized in the name of Jesus Christ means to call upon his name. Peter had just quoted the promise of God in Joel 2:32, 'that whoever calls on the name of the Lord shall be saved.' To believe in Christ is to believe in him as he has been made known in the Scriptures as the Christ (or Messiah) who is the Son of God and the Son of Mary, God made man for us and our salvation, the Christ who died and rose again, mighty to save. It means to lay hold upon all that Christ has done, by faith to stretch out the empty hand and receive the gift of the Holy Spirit to live a different and holy life. To be baptized in the name of Jesus Christ is to submit to this ordinance as an indication that I am laying hold upon the Christ who died on the cross that I might be forgiven.

But if faith is a personal and private commitment of the believing soul to the Saviour, it cannot remain secret. When the crowds asked, 'What shall we do?' Peter did not say, 'Well, here is a decision card; sign it and we will send you some follow-up literature.' He did not say, 'Come to the front of the crowd and I will lead you in saying the sinner's prayer.' No, he has something far better than anything like that. He has something that has not been devised by man, but by our Lord himself. He says, 'Repent and be baptized.'

In his name Peter calls all would-be believers to 'be saved from this perverse generation;' to leave the crowd of Christrejecters and join the church, the company of Christ's believers. Thus we read in verse 41, 'Then those who gladly received his word were baptized; and that day about three thousand souls were *added* to them.' Faith may begin as a private spiritual commitment to Jesus Christ, but it must issue in a public confession of that commitment by obeying the command to be baptized. Peter's command is unconditional. There is no escape clause. No exceptions are allowed. Repent, and let every one of you be baptized. It's a command which brooks no disobedience from those who have repented of their sins and put their faith in Jesus Christ as the only 'name under heaven given among men by which we must be saved' (Acts 4:12).

The sole question that remains is: have you met these conditions for baptism? Have you repented? Repentance means 'to leave the sin I loved before and show that I'm earnest by doing so no more.' And have you put your faith in Christ? Are you trusting in his redeeming blood alone for the remission of your sins, and in his gift of the Holy Spirit to enable you to live in obedience to his commandments? If that is your spiritual state, then there is absolutely nothing to hinder you from being baptized (Acts 8:36).

Chapter Four
The Necessity of Baptism

It is a sad fact that some people who become Christians do not
see the need to be baptized. In reaction to those who lay undue
stress on the necessity of baptism, even daring to assert that
without baptism a person cannot be saved, some Christians
have gone to the other extreme and regarded baptism as
optional or non-essential. Their reasoning usually goes like this:
'I am justified by faith in Christ. What do I need an external
rite like baptism for?' Or it could be just a matter of plain old
pride: 'I couldn't bear to be made a public spectacle of like
that, thank you very much.'

Evangelical Christians, however, cannot at one and the same
time, treat the sacrament of baptism lightly and take the Bible
seriously. Because of the clear command of Christ and the practice of the apostles, it is the plain duty of every professing
Christian to ask for baptism for himself or herself, and of every
Christian minister to press upon his congregation this obligation and privilege.

Let us, then, look a little closer at this matter of the necessity of baptism for every true Christian. To begin with, it's a
necessity because –

Christ commanded his disciples to be baptized

One of the last things Jesus said to the disciples before he ascended to heaven was, 'All authority has been given to me in heaven and on earth. Go therefore and make disciples of all the nations, baptizing them in the name of the Father and of the Son and of the Holy Spirit, teaching them to observe all things that I have commanded you; and lo, I am with you always, even to the end of the age' (Matt. 28:18-20).

In these closing verses of Matthew's Gospel, our Lord asserts his stupendous claim of universal sovereignty. All authority in heaven and on earth has been committed to him. And not until we are convinced of the full authority of the Lord Jesus Christ are we likely to hear and obey his command to be baptized.

Moreover, Christian baptism rests on a divine command which is to be observed in every land and every age until our Lord comes again. This passage clearly states that the three-fold commission to evangelise, baptize and teach applies in its entirety to 'all nations' until the end of time, 'the end of the age'.

Seeing, then, that Christian baptism is commanded by our Lord to be observed universally by the Christian church until he returns in glory, the question of our personal obedience to this command immediately arises. If it is the will of Jesus Christ that every follower or disciple of his should be baptized, then we must bow in submission to his will. We must obey him, not grudgingly, but willingly as those whose delight it is to please the Lord. Before we became Christians we thought only of pleasing ourselves, but now we should always 'make it our aim … to be well pleasing to Him' (2 Cor. 5:9).

Indeed, the whole matter of our obedience to Jesus Christ is really a test of our love for him. He said, 'If you love Me, keep

My commandments' (John 14:15). And again, 'You are My friends if you do whatever I command you' (John 15:14). How willing are we to do what our Lord wants? I tell you, nothing will foster our friendship with Jesus Christ more than willing obedience. And when we discover and obey Christ's command to be baptized, this will bring added joy to our Christian experience. For Jesus said, 'If you know these things, blessed are you if you do them' (John 13:17). A disobedient Christian is a miserable Christian, but those who obey their Lord have great joy in doing so.

But there is something else that is important to understand about this little phrase, 'blessed are you if you do them.' For the main meaning of the word 'blessed' is not 'happy are you if you do them' but, 'blessed (by God) are you if you do them.' Obedience to God's commandments always brings blessing to God's people, especially spiritual blessing. And baptism is a blessing from God in that it brings home to the believer the reality of the cleansing and the new life his soul has received.

So to the question: Is it necessary to be baptized? the answer comes: Is it necessary to have the privilege and blessing that comes with obeying our Lord's ordinance? Why should we want to impoverish ourselves by robbing ourselves of some spiritual blessing? Not the blessing of salvation itself, to be sure, but the blessing of the assurance of salvation that accompanies it. The blessing of feeling accepted by God because we have been accepted into the fellowship of his church.

Baptism is a blessing to those who gladly and believingly submit to it. It is not an onerous burden that has been laid on men's shoulders. It is not a religious shackle which is attached to the gospel. It is our Lord's gracious command, and when a man submits to it, he finds that it is not a duty to which he grudgingly conforms; it is rather one of the gracious privileges and blessings of the gospel which Christ gives to repentant and believing souls.

Secondly, the necessity of baptism is seen in the fact that –

Our Lord himself submitted to this rite

The first recorded step Jesus took in his public ministry was to ask John the Baptist for baptism. It was so important to Jesus that he walked 60 miles (or 100 kilometres) from Nazareth to a place at the River Jordan near to Jerusalem (Mark 1:5,9). As we saw in the first chapter, our Lord did this because he had come to be identified with sinners and to bear away their sin. As the sinner's substitute he submitted to what God required of all sinners. Thus he said to John, who was understandably reluctant to baptize the sinless Son of God, 'It is fitting for us to fulfil all righteousness' – that is, to do all that God requires of men (see Matt. 3:15 NEB.) It was God's will that all Israel should be baptized and enter the kingdom of heaven, and God's own Son, our sin-bearer, claimed no exemption from this divine requirement.

Thus in his baptism, as in his patient suffering on the cross, our Lord was 'leaving an example that (we) should follow His steps' (1 Peter 2:21). It 'became' him who was to endure a deeper baptism of suffering and death, to demonstrate in water baptism his dedication to the will of God, and so give an example to his people. Here, then, is a further incentive to be baptized – not only our Saviour's direct command, but also his personal example. He does not ask us to do what he himself has not done. 'A disciple is not above his teacher, nor a servant above his master. It is enough for a disciple that he be like his teacher, and a servant like his master' (Matt. 10:24-25). Our Lord makes the same point in John 13:13-15, 'You call Me Teacher and Lord, and you say well, for so I am. If I then, your Lord and Teacher, have washed your feet, you also ought to wash one another's feet. For I have given you an example, that you should do as I have done to you.' How much more true is this of our Lord's example of baptism (an enduring ordinance) than of his example of foot-washing (a temporary illustration of Christian humility). Let our response, then be, 'Master, we Thy footsteps follow, we Thy word obey.'

Thirdly, every Christian should regard baptism as necessary because –

It was practised by the apostles

The early disciples did not soft-pedal the issue of baptism. They were men under divine orders. And as we read through the book of Acts, we see how readily those orders were obeyed. Every convert was baptized as soon as possible. In Acts 10:48 we read that Peter 'commanded them to be baptized'. Nowhere did the apostles regard baptism as an optional extra. Whether it was the 3,000 saved on the day of Pentecost (Acts 2:38,41), or the Ethiopian eunuch on a desert road to Gaza (Acts 8:38), or the Philippian jailer who was saved in the early hours of the morning, they were all 'baptized at once' (Acts 16:33). Nowhere does the New Testament envisage a person being converted and not baptized. Like husband and wife, the two (conversion and baptism) were regarded as joined together by God and therefore not to be separated from each other.

To sum up, baptism was obligatory for every Christian in

the early church and there is no valid reason why it should be otherwise today. To be baptized is not a matter of choice or convenience, some trivial rite which can be ignored by those who claim to be Christ's followers. No, it is a command which every Christian must obey: a command given by Christ, emphasised by his own example, and perpetuated by his Church through the centuries. One may go so far as to say that all New Testament churches were 'closed membership' churches; that is to say, all those in fellowship with those churches were baptized believers.

No one who reads the New Testament carefully and prayerfully can escape this conclusion. Paul is able to assume that all believers in the church at Corinth had been admitted by baptism: 'For by one Spirit we were all baptized into one body – whether Jews or Greeks, whether slaves or free' (1 Cor. 12:13). Please notice the past tense ('were all baptized'). Paul is referring to their admission into the body of the church by Spirit and water-baptism; the latter always follows – with one unique exception, (Acts 8:14-17) – the former. As Calvin says, 'Paul, of course, is speaking about the baptism of believers … teaching that part of the meaning of baptism is to bring us into the body of Christ. However, lest anyone might think that the outward symbol itself has power to achieve this, Paul says that it is the Holy Spirit's work.'

Similarly, Paul is able to assume that the Colossian believers were all baptized when he speaks in such general terms of their baptism, saying, 'You were … buried with him in baptism, in which you also were raised with him through faith in the working of God, who raised him from the dead (Col. 2:12). The apostle once again uses water baptism as a symbol of the putting away of the believer's old nature which is the result of Spirit baptism.

George Müller was a man of prayer who, in the nineteenth century, built a string of orphan houses in Bristol and Somerset (England) to the glory of God by simply trusting God for the wherewithal to run them. Well, long after he had been brought to a knowledge of Christ, he began to ask questions about this subject of baptism. So he did something that many others have done, and that is to open the New Testament and work right the way through and look up every reference to the word baptism. And George Müller came to the conclusion that this was part of the gospel call to which he had not given heed. He was baptized and said by way of explanation, 'I am simply doing what I ought to have done years ago!' What about you? 'Why do you delay?' said Ananias to Saul of Tarsus, 'Arise, and be baptized' (Acts 22:16). Is this a question that could be asked of you?

Chapter Five
The Subjects of Baptism (1)

Who should be baptized? What does the Bible teach?

The testimony of Scripture

The New Testament never envisages the baptism of an unbeliever. It always assumes that the recipient is a true believer. Baptism in the New Testament does not precede, but follows, belief in Jesus Christ. We must be converted to Jesus Christ before we can think of confessing him in baptism, otherwise we are putting the cart before the horse. Some selected verses from the book of Acts will help to impress this upon our minds.

Acts 2:41, 'Then those who gladly received his word were baptized.'

Acts 8:12, 'But when they believed Philip as he preached the things concerning the kingdom of God and the name of Jesus Christ, both men and women were baptized.'

Acts 8:36, 'And the eunuch said, "See here is water. What hinders me from being baptized?" Then Philip said, "If you believe with all your heart, you may." And he answered and said, "I believe that Jesus Christ is the Son of God."'

Acts 16:14-15, 'The Lord opened her heart to heed the things spoken by Paul. And she and her household were baptized.'

Acts 16:30-33, '(the Philippian jailer) said, "Sirs, what must I do to be saved?" So they said, "Believe on the Lord Jesus and you will be saved, you and your household" … and immediately he and all his family were baptized.'

Acts 18:8, 'And many of the Corinthians, hearing, believed and were baptized.'

Acts 19:4-5, 'Paul said, "John indeed baptized with a baptism of repentance, saying to the people that they should believe on him who would come after him, that is, on Christ Jesus." When they heard this, they were baptized in the name of the Lord Jesus.'

From these verses it is clear that there is no age limit to who may be baptized. C.H.Spurgeon was baptized at sixteen years of age. Dr.Alexander MacLaren was baptized as a boy of eleven. The age of a candidate for baptism cannot be settled in the abstract. As we have seen, the only requirements are the candidate's personal repentance of sin and confession of faith in Christ, whatever their age. To baptize a person who has not professed faith in Christ is like dressing a man in a uniform and declaring him to be a soldier when he has never enlisted in the Army.

Although the apostles often link baptism with salvation, they never suggest that we can experience a spiritual change of heart just by being baptized. A person is not baptized to make him a Christian, but rather to declare that he is a Christian. It should be obvious that anything that may be done to us outwardly cannot change us inwardly. There are no magical powers in the water. Water can cleanse our hands but not our hearts. Unfortunately, however, many people still think that through being baptized as infants, they automatically become Christians. Their faith is in a particular religious rite, rather than in the redemptive work of Jesus Christ. But in Scripture salvation is by grace through faith and not by any work, whether it be a good deed we perform or a rite to which we submit.

The evidence from church history

Moreover, what Scripture teaches, history affirms. Professor Kurt Aland, in a work entitled, *Did the early church baptize infants?* and A.H.Philpott in an excellent booklet called *Believers' Baptism in the First Four Centuries,* both produce evidence that no case of infant baptism can be proved before AD 200 and that believers' baptism was widely practised at the end of the 4th century.

Tertullian's *De Baptismo* (Concerning Baptism) contains the first explicit reference in all Christian writing, Scripture included, to the practice of infant baptism; and significantly it is a protest against it. Indeed, he argues for the 'deferment of baptism ... as regards children ... It is true our Lord says, Forbid them not to come to me. So let them come when they are growing up, when they are learning, when they are being taught what they are coming to: let them be made Christians when they have become competent to know Christ ... Let them first learn how to ask for salvation, so that you may be seen to have given to one that asketh ... All who understand what a burden baptism is will have more fear of obtaining it than of its postponement. Faith unimpaired has no doubt of its salvation'

(XVIII.19-34). Written about AD 195, Tertullian's *De Baptismo* can hardly be taken as a protest against a practice going back to the apostles themselves. It seems much more probable to see it as a protest against a new development taking place throughout the church at the turn of the third century.

This is substantiated by the fact that the only two other descriptions of baptism during the second century which we have support believers' baptism as the recognised practice. The first of these is found in the *Didache* or Teaching of the Twelve Apostles, a manual of uncertain date which most scholars agree displays the character of a very primitive Christian community. In the *Didache* baptism was administered only when the candidates had 'first recited all these things'. That is, all things concerning the Way of Life and the Way of Death, the subject matter of the manual (*Didache*, VII.1.). This would exclude infants and little children.

The other account of baptism is in the *First Apology* of Justin Martyr written about the middle of the second century. As his name implies, he died a martyr in Rome about AD 163. According to Justin, baptism is given only to 'as many as are persuaded and believe that the things are true which are taught by the church and undertake to be able to live accordingly' (*First Apology, 61*). This again implies a period of instruction and probation beforehand which would exclude infants and very young children.

However, the situation began to change in the third century, with Hippolytus in the West and Origen in the East both advocating infant baptism as a practice which derived its origin and authority from the apostles. In a document called the *Apostolic Tradition* (about AD 220) Hippolytus alludes to it as an 'unquestioned rule'. He says, 'First you should baptize the little ones. All who can speak for themselves should speak. But for those who cannot speak, their parents should speak, or another who belongs to the family,' *(Apostolic Tradition, 21).* Although baptism in this document is accompanied by interrogation and an affirmation of belief in the clauses of the Apostles' Creed, sponsors are permitted to speak for those too young to respond for themselves.

This reference to parents or relatives professing faith and promising allegiance to Christ on behalf of infants was not altogether new. Thirty years before the publication of Hippolytus' *Apostolic Tradition,* Tertullian had rejected the idea, saying, 'What need is there (if babies should not be baptized) for their sponsors to be brought into peril, seeing they may possibly themselves fail of their promises by death, or be deceived by the subsequent development of an evil disposition? *(De Baptismo XVIII.19-34).* But by the fifth century things took a decided turn in favour of infant baptism. At the council of Carthage (AD 411) sixty seven bishops from North Africa decided unanimously not to defer baptism until the eighth day, as in circumcision, but to baptize directly after birth.

So from the middle of the third century to the end of the fifth century, believers' baptism and infant baptism were both practised in the church, with infant baptism slowly gaining in popularity until it was universally accepted. But Johannes Warns (*Baptism,* ch. IV, Paternoster Press, 1962) cites many eminent church fathers who, even as late as the fifth century, were baptized as believers despite the fact that they were the children of bishops or of long-established Christian homes.

He lists Eusebius of Caesarea (a church historian, died about AD 340), Ambrose (Bishop of Milan, died 397), Gregory (Bishop of Nazianzen, died 390), Basil the Great (Bishop of Caesarea in Cappadocia, died 379), Chrysostom (a great church orator who died 407), Rufinus (a great translator 410), Jerome (the ablest scholar the Western church could boast, died 420), and Augustine (the most renowned theologian of his time, died 430). Why did their Christian parents not baptize them as children? Why was baptism delayed till after conversion? Does this not show that infant baptism only gained in popularity as the church became more and more removed in time from the original practice of the apostles?

Before we leave the evidence of church history, we should deal with the case for infant baptism that is often made from Polycarp's words at his martyrdom in AD 155. 'Eighty six years I have served him, and he has done me no wrong. How can I blaspheme my King who saved me?' It is argued that if Polycarp was baptized when he was fourteen years old, he would have been one hundred when he died. Not many people reached that age in those days! Therefore Polycarp was almost certainly baptized as a baby eighty six years before his martyrdom. But this is a fallacious argument because we do not know how old he was when he died. If he was healthy enough to serve Christ eighty six years, there is good reason to believe he could have lived to ninety six. The apostle John lived into his late nineties. Polycarp, therefore, could have been baptized as a believer at the age of eight or ten.

Scriptural objections to infant baptism

Several objections to infant baptism may be drawn from Scripture.

(1) Scripture is the church's sole authority

Many churches practise infant baptism because it is an old tradition of the Christian church and they believe that Scripture and tradition are to be received as of equal worth. But Jesus taught that Scripture is sufficient in itself as our guide to faith and conduct, and must be regarded as supreme over tradition. Why? Because Scripture is the Word of God, and our duty is rather to 'keep' or 'hold' God's Word and if necessary 'lay aside' the traditions of men. Traditions as Jesus told the Pharisees can be elevated above the Word of God: 'Laying aside the commandment of God, you hold the tradition of men … making the word of no effect through your tradition which you have handed down.' (Mark 7:8,13).

(2) There is no command in Scripture to baptize infants

It is generally argued that the apostles, being Jews, would have naturally wanted to baptize infants since they practised infant circumcision. If our Lord had not intended this, he would have specifically forbidden it. This line of reasoning, however, is fraught with difficulties. If the apostles were accustomed to baptizing infants (an assumption based on an argument from silence), why did they prevent Jewish mothers from bringing their babies to Jesus for his blessing? (Matt. 19:13-15; Mark 10:13-16; Luke 18:15-17).

They were actively engaged in a baptizing ministry under Christ's supervision (John 3:22; 4:1-2) and were even baptizing more disciples than John who was himself baptizing large numbers (Mark 1:5). So if they were predisposed to baptizing infants, they would naturally have welcomed these babies and not rejected them. But the fact that they did try to turn them away shows that they, like John, only baptized those old enough to repent and believe.

To be honest, this incident of Jesus blessing the children has nothing whatever to do with baptism. As Spurgeon pointed out, we might as well prove that Jesus vaccinated them as prove that he applied water to them (Sermon 581 on Mark 10:13-16). To accept the importance of little children in Christ's sight and pray for his blessing upon them, does not mean that we have to baptize them.

It is also important to notice that the main emphasis of the story (as made plain in Mark 10:15) is on the necessity of receiving the good news of the kingdom of God 'like a child'. That is, with the absolute trust and simplicity with which a child accepts the word of its parents or superiors. Our Lord is not saying that the kingdom of God belongs to children simply because they are young and innocent. If that were so, we would have a mandate from this text to baptize all children, even those of unbelievers. But this is surely not what Jesus meant. He is simply saying that children belong to the kingdom only if they 'come' to him in simple trust to 'receive' it. And in this, of course, little children are an example to us all. For unless we assume the position of a child before our Creator and come to Christ in simple trust and dependence for God's kingdom, we shall not enter it.

As for the analogy between baptism and circumcision, it does have certain limitations. It is true that circumcision was the initiatory rite into the old covenant which God made with Israel while baptism is the initiatory rite into the new covenant which God made with the church, the new Israel. But the basis for membership in the new covenant is not the same as that for the old. The old covenant was made with a particular nation, Israel. Entrance into this covenant was by physical descent and so every male Israelite child and the children of slaves (Gen. 17:12) was given the sign of incorporation, namely circumcision. It was this that designated him an Israelite in contrast to Gentiles who were 'the uncircumcised'.

This is further substantiated by the fact that in the old covenant circumcision was administered to older children and to adults regardless of whether or not they were true believers in God. Thus circumcision was administered to Ishmael as a teenager even though God assured Abraham that he would not be a partaker of the spiritual blessings promised to his father (Gen. 17:18-27). Again, in Joshua 5 God commands his servant to see that the entire nation be circumcised because none of the males born in the forty years of wandering in the wilderness had been. Yet many of the people still served false gods (Joshua 24:14-15). There was no concern for personal faith. Circumcision was never withheld because the child or his parents had no faith.

The new covenant, however, is not made with ethnic groups or families because the new birth is not dependent on heredity, but on the regenerating work of the Holy Spirit. This is made so clear in John 1:12-13, 'But as many as received Him, to them he gave the right to become children of God, to those who believe in His name: who were born, not of blood, nor of the will of the flesh, nor of the will of man, but of God.' The new covenant is made with individuals who believe, and its radius is the world. Moreover, we cannot identify the elect with the children of believers, for we do not know whom God has chosen. But we do know that those who are his are marked by an experience of inward grace and personal faith, and that such were the New Testament candidates for baptism, whether they were children of believers or not.

(3) There is no evidence in Scripture for infant baptism

It is true that in the book of Acts, Luke records a number of household baptisms (11:14, 16:15, 16:33, 18:8; see also 1 Cor. 1:16). But except in the case of Lydia, statements are made giving clear evidence that these households consisted of responsible persons who could hear the word, believe, speak in tongues, rejoice in God and serve the saints. One example will suffice: 'Crispus, the ruler of the synagogue, believed in the Lord with all his household ... and were baptized' (Acts 18:8). The argument from silence in Lydia's case is, in the words of the Swiss theologian Karl Barth, a very 'thin thread' on which to hang infant baptism. For while Lydia may have been a widow, she could equally have been unmarried, and in charge of a household of servants who assisted her in her trade as 'a seller of purple goods' (Acts 16:14). Infant baptism can be found here only by those most anxious to do so.

Great importance is also laid on 1 Corinthians 7:14 where Paul says that the children of a mixed marriage in which one partner is a believer and the other is not, are 'holy'. This, it is argued, is the normal New Testament designation for believers, and as such these children are therefore entitled to baptism. But as two Anglican commentators, Robertson and Plummer, assert, 'the verse throws no light on the question of infant baptism' (*I.C.C. Commentary on 1 Corinthians*). And for this simple reason: the term 'holy' which is applied to infants, is also applied to the unbelieving partner who is said to be 'sanctified'. Should he not then be baptized too? The answer, of course, is No, for in the next two verses Paul insists that such partners are 'unbelieving' and need to be 'saved'.

Clearly, the word 'holy' cannot justify the baptism of infants or unbelieving children. Paul was dealing with another issue altogether. Should a Christian leave an unbelieving spouse? Is there not some uncleanness in such a union? No, says Paul, the relationship is hallowed in God's sight and the children are not unclean or illegitimate.

The words of Peter in Acts 2:39 are sometimes used to support the practice of infant baptism: 'The promise is to you and to your children,' referring to God's offer of forgiveness of sins and the gift of the Holy Spirit. But the emphasis here is not on the children as being in a special class because they are children of believers. Rather, the phrase, 'and to your children' means that the promise is for all subsequent generations. Likewise the phrase, 'and to all who are afar off' means that the promise is also for people of every nation. But is the promise of the remission of sins and the gift of the Holy Spirit made indiscriminately to every person in every nation and of every generation? No, it is not. For the apostle qualifies his statement by saying, 'For the promise is to you and to … as many as the Lord our God will call.'

It is God's summons to them which causes them to call upon the name of the Lord and be saved (verse 21). How can infants hear the call of God and respond in personal repentance and faith? They can't. These words of the apostle Peter do not give us licence to baptize any person in our family or in a faraway land who has not been effectually called by the Holy Spirit and cried out, 'What shall we do?' (verse 37).

Spurgeon summed it up well: 'If we could find (infant baptism) in the Word of God, we should adopt it. It would help us out of a great difficulty, for it would take away from us that reproach which is attached to us – that we are odd and do not as other people do. But we have looked well through the Bible and cannot find it, and do not believe it is there; nor do we believe that others can find infant baptism in the Scriptures, unless they themselves first put it there'

(4) If the absence of faith excludes from the Lord's Supper, it excludes also from baptism

The category of baptized but non-communicant church members is completely absent from the New Testament. Indeed, judged by New Testament standards, it is an absurdity. Surely if infants are qualified for baptism and admission to the church, there is no biblical warrant for excluding them from the Lord's Table. In Acts 2 the pattern is that those who were baptized continued in fellowship and in the breaking of bread. If we are to be consistent, then we should exclude infants from baptism as well because of lack of faith, for faith is more often linked with baptism than it is with the Lord's Supper.

In the old covenant, children came to the Passover meal at a very young age, (see Exodus 12:26), and it is to the credit of Eastern Orthodox churches that baptized infants and children receive communion regularly even while they are still in arms. Now some Anglicans are recognising the need for consistency. Michael Green says, 'The child who is not allowed to partake in the holy communion with its parents can be made to feel a second-class citizen in the life of the church, and isolated from his parents … I believe we must grasp the nettle firmly and maintain both that baptism is the rite of entry (into the church) and that children who have been baptized may take their share in the holy communion with their parents.'

This is a commendable attempt to be consistent, but there are serious objections to be raised against it. First, as Calvin long ago pointed out, communion is not a sacrament for infants (*Institutes* IV. xvi.30). Those who partake are required to examine themselves beforehand according to 1 Corinthians 11:27-32: 'Therefore whoever eats this bread or drinks this cup of the Lord in an unworthy manner will be guilty of the body and blood of the Lord. But let a man examine himself, and so let him eat of the bread and drink of the cup. For he who eats and drinks in an unworthy manner eats and drinks judgement to himself, not discerning the Lord's body. For this reason many are weak and sick among you, and many sleep. For if we would judge ourselves, we would not be judged. But when we are judged, we are chastened by the Lord, that we may not be condemned with the world.' Since little children are incapable of examining themselves it follows that they should not receive communion.

Secondly, if little children are brought up to believe that by virtue of their baptism they are Christians in the full sense of the word, and if they are strengthened in that belief week by week in partaking of holy communion, who would ever be able to persuade them of their need to be born again and converted to Christ? What a sad day it would be if those who baptize infants lost their evangelical message in their efforts to gain theological consistency!

If faith is absent, baptism and communion must wait. To quote Spurgeon again, 'I consider that baptism of an unconscious infant is just as foolish as the baptism of a ship or bell, for there is as much Scripture for the one as for the other.'

Chapter Six
The Subjects of Baptism (2)

Many Reformed Christians who practise infant baptism do so on the basis of what is termed 'covenant theology'. We must now examine their case.

The argument of covenant theology

The religion of the Bible is not only revealed religion but covenant religion. Indeed, we cannot really understand the Bible unless we see it as the revelation of God's gracious purposes for and dealings with those people he is calling out of the world for himself. For since Adam and Eve alienated the human race from God by their fall into sin, God has sought to rescue and reconcile men to himself. And the basis on which God deals with the people whom he purposes to redeem is his covenant of grace containing the promise, 'I will be your God and you shall be my people.' This covenant slogan is found throughout the Bible (Gen. 17:7-14; Exod. 19:4-6; Lev. 26:12; Deut. 7:6, 14:2; Jer. 7:23, 11:4, 24:7, 30:22, 31:33, 32:38; Ezek. 11:20, 36:28; Zech. 8:8, 13:9; 2 Cor. 6:16; Rev. 21:3).

(1) The unity of the Bible and the covenant of grace

The word covenant is a legal term for any binding undertaking. When used in Scripture to describe what God has done, however, it is not to be thought of as an agreement between two equal parties. It is more like a testament or will in which the testator has sole and entire discretion in the disposal of his own estate. The Greek word *diathēkē* can mean either, and in Galatians 3:15-18 and Hebrews 9:15-18 there is a play on the two meanings of the word, in order to make it plain that God's covenant is a 'last will and testament' in which he has freely made certain promises. Hence, too, the two parts of the Bible are known as the Old and New 'Testaments'.

Now the covenant promises are not unconditional, since God's people are required to respond in adoring trust and obedience. This is their part of the covenant. But it is God himself who lays down the conditions as well as the benefits.This is how it has always been. God's grace: all of him for us. And our faith: all of us for him. Such is the covenant which runs right through Scripture. So the two parts of the Bible should not be regarded as records of separate covenants made by God with mankind, but as records of how the one covenant of grace was administered in two different ways during the age of promise and the age of fulfilment.

Support for this view goes right back to Abraham when God took the initiative and approached him in sheer grace, promising that in him 'all the families of the earth shall be blessed' (Gen. 12:1-3). God also promised to multiply his descendants 'as the stars of the heaven and as the sand which is on the seashore' (Gen. 22:17) and to give him 'all the land of Canaan, as an everlasting possession' (Gen. 17:8). To this covenant Abraham responded in faith. 'And he believed in the

LORD; and He accounted it to him for righteousness' (Gen. 15:6). The grace of God was met by the faith of Abraham.

This is how Abraham was justified before God. It was not a reward due to good works, but a 'gift' offered to him because he trusted 'Him who justifies the ungodly', a phrase which occurs in Romans 4:1-5, 'What then shall we say that Abraham our father has found according to the flesh? For if Abraham was justified by works, he has something to boast about, but not before God. For what does the Scripture say? "Abraham believed God, and it was accounted to him for righteousness." Now to him who works, the wages are not counted as grace but as debt. But to him who does not work but believes on him who justifies the ungodly, his faith is accounted for righteousness.'

And that is how we too are put right with God. There is no other way. There never has been. Let us put away for good the erroneous idea that salvation was by keeping the law in Old Testament times, but now it is by faith in God's promises of salvation. Men and women were saved in the Old Testament in just the same way as they were saved in the New Testament: by the unmerited favour of God's grace to which we respond in adoring trust and obedience.

In Galatians 3:6-29 Paul explains why God gave the law to Moses for men to keep 430 years after he made his covenant of grace with Abraham. It was not to annul the covenant made with Abraham and so 'make the promise (of salvation by faith) of no affect' (verse 17). Law keeping cannot establish any claims on God, because the law demands one hundred per cent obedience. So instead of commending us to God, the law condemns us as transgressors and brings us 'under the curse' (verses.10-14).

Why, then, was it given? 'It was added because of transgressions, till the Seed should come to whom the promise was made' (verse 19). Notice the two reasons. First, the purpose of the law was not to contradict what God had already promised to Abraham and to 'those who are of faith (who) are the sons of Abraham' (verse 7), but to prepare them to receive what he freely offers 'to those who believe' (verse 22). And secondly, the way the law sought to do this was to convict all of sin and convince them of the utter futility of trying to earn God's favour and approval by their own works of law-keeping. 'But the Scripture has confined all under sin, that the promise by faith in Jesus Christ might be given to those who believe' (verse 22).

The giving of the law, then, was not another way of salvation, but a provisional enactment in God's dealings with men to govern them in their spiritual infancy, until they were ready to enter into the full benefits of his covenant of grace through Christ. 'The law was our tutor to bring us to Christ, that we might be justified by faith. But after faith has come, we are no longer under a tutor. For you are all sons of God through faith in Christ Jesus' (verses 24-26).

So when the law had done its work, it became 'obsolete' (Heb. 8:13). The restriction of grace to one nation (the Jews), and its insistence on animal sacrifices and on the temple as the only place of worship, and its special regulations regarding clean and unclean food, also became obsolete. But God's covenant of grace through faith did not become obsolete. It was not discontinued because it is the supreme covenant governing God's dealings with men from Abraham's day to our own. It is called 'new' only in the sense that what was originally promised to Abraham has at last found its fulfilment in and through Christ whose blood alone can cleanse us from all sin, and whose Spirit can write God's law into every believing heart.

Jeremiah prophesied that God would make a new covenant: 'Behold, the days are coming, says the LORD, when I will make a new covenant with the house of Israel and with the house of Judah – not according to the covenant that I made with their fathers in the day that I took them by the hand to lead them out of the land of Egypt, My covenant which they broke, though I was a husband to them, says the LORD. But this is the covenant that I will make with the house of Israel after those days, says the LORD: I will put My law in their minds, and write it on their hearts; and I will be their God, and they shall be My people. No more shall every man teach his neighbour, and every man his brother, saying, "Know the LORD", for they all shall know Me, from the least of them to the greatest of them, says the LORD. For I will forgive their iniquity, and their sin I will remember no more.' (31:31-34).

Ezekiel, like Jeremiah, emphasises the inwardness of the new covenant: 'Then I will sprinkle clean water on you, and you shall be clean; I will cleanse you from all your filthiness and from all your idols. I will give you a new heart and put a new spirit within you; I will take the heart of stone out of your flesh and give you a heart of flesh. I will put My Spirit within you and cause you to walk in My statutes, and you will keep My judgements and do them' (36:25-27).

In this respect the new covenant is not only new, but everlasting. Nothing needs to be added to it (as was the case with the old covenant, which was still looking forward to the coming of Christ and the gift of his Spirit). But it is not new in the sense that it is discontinuous with the old. God has not changed his way of salvation.

The whole argument of Hebrews 9 rests on the fact that God's covenant is also a will and that a will is not effective without the death of the testator. Accordingly, God's will or covenant did not reach its full effectiveness until the animal sacrifices of the Old Testament era were replaced by the sacrifice of the Lord Jesus himself on Calvary. But it remains the same covenant of grace with only one way of salvation, whereby sinful man puts his trust in the God who, at enormous personal cost, acquits the ungodly.

The unity of God's plan of salvation is further proved by the fact that in both testaments the covenant is administered by word and sacraments, and that although the sacraments differ in the two testaments, they correspond to each other and, together with the word, testify of Christ.

Thus the Old Testament sacrament of initiation into the covenant was circumcision, and this is replaced by baptism in the New. Indeed, in his letter to the Colossians, Paul brings the two sacramental acts together and links them with the dying and rising of Christ. 'In Him you were also circumcised with the circumcision made without hands, by putting off the body of the sins of the flesh, by the circumcision of Christ; buried with Him in baptism, in which you also were raised with Him through faith in the working of God, who raised Him from the dead' (Col. 2:11-12).

Similarly, the celebration of the covenant in the Passover meal of the Old Testament finds its New Testament equivalent in the Lord's Supper. Passover speaks of Christ. 'Christ, our Passover, was sacrificed for us' (1 Cor. 5:7). And the Lord's Supper corresponds to the Passover meal because it is a sacrament of the new covenant in Christ's blood (1 Cor. 11:25). Both ordinances portray the great spiritual truth of redemption by the shed blood of an innocent victim in the sinner's place.

(2) The implication of the link between circumcision and baptism

If there is only one covenant of grace throughout the Bible offering salvation only to those who believe, how does it relate to the children of believers? We must now turn our attention to this question as we seek to determine who should be baptized. From the time of the Reformation upholders of infant baptism have argued that just as infants were circumcised under the Abrahamic covenant (Gen.17), so now the infants of believers should be baptized under the new covenant. They agree that Abraham was justified by faith as an adult and his response to the grace of God was sealed afterwards with circumcision, the sign of the covenant (just like believers' baptism). But they point out that Isaac was born into the covenant community, and he received the seal of circumcision long before he could make any response to God's grace. 'Abraham circumcised his son Isaac when he was eight days old, as God had commanded him' (Gen. 21:4). This tells us, they argue, that the child born into a believing home has the right to receive the sign of belonging to God's people, even when he or she is too young to fulfil the conditions on which the covenant was made with his believing parents.

Here, then, is a pertinent question. If infants were admitted into the Old Testament church, are they to be excluded from the New Testament church? Does the church consist only of those who are old enough to profess faith? The answer of the New Testament is an emphatic 'yes'.

The fundamental flaw in the argument of those who baptize infants, on the basis of covenant theology, is that they read the New Testament into the Old without proper attention to the progressive nature of God's revelation in Scripture and the difference between the administration of his covenant in the age of promise and its administration in the age of fulfilment. For in the age of promise the blessings of the covenant had to be couched in national and material terms which the people could understand and lay hold of. So the promised seed of Abraham was physical (the Jews) and the inheritance he was to receive was earthly (Canaan).

It is only in the New Testament that God fully reveals that Abraham's true seed (to whom the promises of grace are made) are not his children by physical birth, but his children by spiritual re-birth. 'Therefore know that only those who are of faith are sons of Abraham. And the Scripture, foreseeing that God would justify the Gentiles by faith, preached the gospel to Abraham beforehand, saying, "In you all the nations shall be blessed." So then those who are of faith are blessed with believing Abraham' (Gal. 3:7-9. See also Rom. 2:28-29).

Likewise, his real inheritance is not to be the land of Canaan but eternal life with God in the new Jerusalem. 'By faith Abraham obeyed when he was called to go out to the place which he would receive as an inheritance. And he went out, not knowing where he was going. By faith he dwelt in the land of promise as in a foreign country, dwelling in tents with Isaac and Jacob, the heirs with him of the same promise; for he waited for the city which has foundations, whose builder and maker is God' (Heb. 11:8-10).

So if we want to understand the link between circumcision and baptism, we must bear in mind this distinction between the form of the covenant of grace in the Old Testament and its form in the New. The fact that it was originally applied in physical terms to Abraham's blood descendants (and to those brought with his money) explains why circumcision was performed shortly after birth and why it was performed on the organ of generation.

But when the promises of the covenant of grace reached their full spiritual significance with the coming of Christ, the sign of the covenant could obviously not remain the same. To portray accurately the new spiritual nature of the membership of the covenant people of God, the sign of circumcision was replaced with the sign of baptism. For baptism highlights *regeneration* rather than generation as the door into the church; and the gift of the Holy Spirit received by faith as the cause of this regeneration rather than the human organ of generation.

To those who argue that as Abraham was required to circumcise his seed, so believers must now have their children baptized, Spurgeon replies: 'Now some observe the type and interpret it not according to prejudice but according to Scripture – in the type the seed of Abraham is circumcised – you draw the inference that all typified by the seed of Abraham ought to be baptized, and I do not cavil at the conclusion, but I ask you, who are the true seed of Abraham? Paul answers in Romans 4:8, 'They which are the children of the flesh, these are not the children of God; but the children of the promise are counted for the seed. As many as believe on the Lord Jesus Christ, whether they be Jews or Gentiles, are Abraham's seed. Whether eight days old in grace, or more or less, everyone of Abraham's seed has a right to baptism, but I deny that the unregenerate, whether children or adults, are of the spiritual seed of Abraham' (*Metropolitan Tabernacle Pulpit, XIV, pp 695-6*).

Baptism, therefore, should only be administered to those who become Abraham's children by this spiritual birth. It should not be administered to the physical children of believers because covenant privilege is no longer tied to blood as it was in the age of type and shadow. John 1:12-13, categorically says that Christ gave the right to become children of God only to those 'who believed on his name, who were born, not of blood, nor of the will of the flesh, nor of the will of man, but of God.' To insist that the blessings of the covenant of grace can be promised to the children of believers in virtue of their physical descent from their parents is to take a step backwards into the Old Testament. It is to ignore the overwhelming teaching of the New Testament that since the coming of Christ, God's dealings with men are no longer based on physical descent but on spiritual rebirth.

The first one to draw attention to this was John the Baptist. When he saw many of the Pharisees and Sadducees coming for baptism, he said to them, 'Brood of vipers! Who warned you to flee from the wrath to come. Therefore bear fruits worthy of repentance, and do not think to say to yourselves, "We have Abraham as our father," for I say to you that God is able to raise up children to Abraham from these stones.' (Matt. 3:7-9).

Our Lord also criticised the Scribes and Pharisees for assuming that mere physical descent was enough to make them the children of God. 'I know that you are Abraham's descendants, but you seek to kill Me, because My word has no place in you ... If you were Abraham's children you would do the works of Abraham (he believed God's word and acted on it). But now you seek to kill Me, a man who has told you the truth which I heard from God ... you are of your father the devil, and the desires of your father you want to do' (John 8:37-44).

It is Paul, however, who most clearly dismisses this illusion. In Romans 9:6-8 he writes: 'For they are not all Israel who are of Israel, nor are they all children because they are the seed of Abraham ... those who are children of the flesh are not the children of God; but the children of the promise are counted as the seed.' Again, in Galatians 3:7-9, Paul says, 'Only those who are of faith (i.e. men who believe God's promise in Christ of salvation) are sons of Abraham. And the Scripture, foreseeing that God would justify the Gentiles by faith, preached the gospel to Abraham beforehand, saying, "In you all the nations shall be blessed." So then, those who are of faith are blessed with believing Abraham.' The crucial words, however, are contained in verse 16. 'Now to Abraham and his Seed were the promises made. He does not say, "And to seeds", as of many, but as of one, "and to your Seed", who is Christ.' This is a staggering statement! The blessing of salvation which God promised to Abraham was promised not to his natural descendants, but to Christ and to all those who believe in Christ.

The blessing can only come through Christ because (verses 13-14), 'Christ has redeemed us from the curse of the law, having become a curse for us ... that the blessing of Abraham might come upon the Gentiles in Christ Jesus, that we might receive the promise of the Spirit through faith.' Now 'there is neither Jew nor Greek, there is neither slave nor free, there is neither male nor female; for you are all one in Christ Jesus. And if you are Christ's, then you are Abraham's offspring, heirs according to promise.' (verses 28-29).

Could words be any plainer? The sign and seal of the covenant of grace can only be given to those who 'are Christ's' (verse 29); to 'those who are of faith (who) are sons of Abraham' (v.7); 'to those who believe' (verse 22). It is our spiritual relationship to Christ by faith that brings us into the covenant of grace, and not our physical relationship to believing parents by blood.

Inclusion within the covenant of grace cannot be secured on the grounds of the faith of believing parents; nor can the unbelief of parents deprive their children of membership, if they are among the elect of God. The only blood that qualifies us for inclusion in the covenant of grace and permits us to receive the sacraments of baptism and the Lord's Supper, is the 'blood of Jesus' which cleanses us the moment we confess our sin and put our trust in him to save us. 'If we walk in the light as He is in the light, we have fellowship with one another, and the blood of Jesus Christ His Son cleanses us from all sin. If we say that we have no sin, we deceive ourselves, and the truth is not in us. If we confess our sins, He is faithful and just to forgive us our sins and to cleanse us from all unrighteousness.' (1 John 1:7-9).

(3) The position of the children of believers

What, then, is the position of infants and young children who belong to Christian parents? Are they worse off under the new covenant than they were under the old? By no means! Although they are not to be enrolled in the official membership of the church and recognised as Christians, they are to be included in the community of the church. And that means that to all practical intents and purposes they are spiritually better off than the children of Old Testament believers.

First, because in the church today the Holy Spirit has a greater and more powerful ministry than he ever had before Christ came. Jesus said as much in John 14:16-17: 'And I will pray the Father, and He will give you another Helper, that He may abide with you forever – the Spirit of truth, whom the world cannot receive, because it neither sees Him nor knows Him; but you know Him, for he dwells with you and will be in you.' And again, in John 16:8-15: 'And when He has come, He will convict the world of sin, and of righteousness, and of judge-ment: of sin, because they do not believe in Me; of righteous-ness, because I go to My Father and you see Me no more; of judgement, because the ruler of this world is judged. I still have many things to say to you, but you cannot bear them now. However, when He, the Spirit of truth, has come, He will guide you into all truth; for He will not speak on His own authority, but whatever He hears He will speak; and He will tell you things to come. He will glorify Me, for He will take of what is Mine and declare it to you. All things that the Father has are Mine. Therefore I said that He will take of Mine and declare it you.'

Second, children of believers are more privileged than children of Old Testament believers because God's way of salvation is preached more fully and clearly in the church and taught in Christian homes than it could ever be under the old covenant. They live in the age of fulfilment, not in the era of types and shadows.

To withhold baptism from children until they personally come to Christ in repentance and faith does not diminish one bit their exposure to the gracious saving influences of the Holy Spirit and the Word of God and the worship of his name. Conversely, neither does it increase their experience of the grace of God to baptize them before they come to Christ. Indeed, it is more likely to be a hindrance to them, giving them a false sense of spiritual security as it has done to many millions down the centuries. So let Christian parents do what Aristides tells us Christians of the second century did when they 'gave thanks to God for their new-born babes'. Let them be nurtured and taught within a prayerful community of believers and a godly home. Let parents claim them in prayer. But let them come to repentance and faith in the right time and manner, as the Holy Spirit shall enlighten them. And let baptism be for them, as for others, what the New Testament shows it to be – the solemn, joyous, intelligent confession of union with Christ made in the midst of the church by those who know in whom they have believed.

Chapter Seven
The Mode of Baptism

The manner or mode of baptism is as important as the manner or mode of the Lord's Supper. They are both symbolic ordinances. That is to say they employ outward and visible signs of inward and spiritual realities. The central truths of our salvation are portrayed in them, and as such they must accurately portray the gospel of the grace of God. Just as the believer must eat broken bread and drink poured out wine to signify his active participation by faith in the saving benefits of Christ's atoning death, so must he be immersed in water to signify that he has been united with Christ in his death, burial and resurrection. The mode of baptism is, therefore, a matter of primary significance and not a mere secondary detail to be determined largely by convenience or personal taste. What, then, is our basis for believing that the New Testament teaches that baptism should be by immersion? Well, first:

The meaning of the Greek verb *baptizo* demands immersion

The verb which is used in the Greek New Testament for 'to baptize' is *baptizō*, and according to the *Dictionary of New Testament Theology* (Vol.1, p.144), the primary meaning of the word is to dip, immerse or submerge. The Greeks used it to describe the dyeing of a garment or the drawing of water by dipping a cup into a bowl. Just as it was necessary to immerse the entire garment if it was to be completely dyed, so it was necessary to put the whole cup beneath the water to fill it. The word was often used of a ship that had been sunk or of a person hopelessly submerged in debt. In the Septuagint (the Greek translation of the Old Testament), it is used of Naaman dipping himself seven times in the river Jordan (2 Kings 5:14). Luke also uses it of our Lord's blood-baptism at the cross when, as our sin-bearer, his soul would be immersed in the deep waters of suffering and divine chastisement (Luke 12:50; Isaiah 53:5).

The word *baptizō* is never used to signify pouring or sprinkling for the simple reason that those actions have their own specific words, namely, *ekcheō,* meaning I pour, and *rhantizō,* meaning I sprinkle. Even to Greek-speaking people today *baptizō* has only one meaning, and that is to immerse. It should therefore not come as a surprise that the Greek Orthodox church baptizes its infants by immersion. Their knowledge of their own language has preserved the correctness of their mode of baptism even though tradition has supplanted the biblical requirement that only believers qualify for immersion.

But if this is so, why did the translators of the Authorised Version not translate the word *baptizō* as immerse instead of as baptize? Well, when the Authorised Version scholars were doing their great work of revision, they originally did translate the word *baptizō* by the word dip. But realising the far-reaching consequences, they decided eventually to transliterate and leave the Greek word in an anglicised form (baptize) so that every man could interpret it as he wanted to. Thus, through their indecision or reluctance to translate the word *baptizō* properly, the erroneous practice of sprinkling has been maintained.

The grammar of the New Testament allows only for immersion

The fact that the word *baptizō* is never used in the passive voice with water as its subject confirms our conclusion that its meaning is to immerse. Water is never said to be baptized upon a man, which is what we would expect if the idea of sprinkling were involved. Rather, the New Testament speaks of a person being baptized 'into' water. For instance, in Mark 1:9 we read, 'In those days Jesus came from Nazareth of Galilee and was baptized by John in the Jordan.' The preposition used here ('in the Jordan') is the Greek preposition *eis* and can only mean 'into' – the river Jordan being the element into which our Lord was immersed when he was baptized. To speak of dipping someone in the river is expressive enough, but to speak of dipping them into it, is even more so.

Again, in Mark 1:5 we read, 'Then all the land of Judea ... went out to him and were all baptized by him in the Jordan river;' and in verse 8, 'I indeed baptized you with water, but he will baptize you with the Holy Spirit.' In both these verses the preposition used is not *eis* but *en* which, with the dative, can only mean in, not with. John did not baptize his converts *with* the river Jordan, but *in* the river Jordan. Likewise in verse 8 the literal sense is, 'I baptized you in water, but he will baptize you in the Holy Spirit.' Dr. Plummer (an Anglican) in his commentary on Matthew (3:11) says, 'It is his (John's) office to bind them to a new life symbolised by immersion in water. But one far mightier, whose bond-servant he is unworthy to be, is coming to immerse them in an element far more potent – the Holy Spirit and fire' (p.28).

To sum up, the use of the prepositions *en* and *eis* show clearly the absurdity of trying to translate the verb *baptizō* as sprinkle or pour, for both convey the idea of being baptized in or into the water. And to quote Herbert Carson (who seceded from the Church of England in 1964 partly because of this issue), 'You can dip someone in the water, but you cannot sprinkle them into the water, unless you have used a mincer beforehand.'

The descriptions of baptism in the New Testament suggest immersion

There are two main accounts of baptisms in the New Testament: the baptism of Jesus and the baptism of the Ethiopian eunuch: Matthew 3:16: 'When He had been baptized, Jesus came up immediately from the water ... ' and Acts 8:38,39: 'Both Philip and the eunuch went down into the water, and he baptized him. Now when they came up out of the water ... '

Now in each instance the baptizer and the baptized went deep into the river for the ceremony to take place. Why? To obtain sufficient depth of water for the candidate to be immersed. If sprinkling was the method, the baptizer could easily have performed the operation with a basin of water. After all, those who baptize by sprinkling today do not need to stand in a river or a bath for the purpose. All that is required is a very small amount of water.

Added to this, of course, is the significant comment in John's Gospel about the location of John the Baptist's ministry. 'John also was baptising in Aenon near Salim, because there was much water there' (John 3:23). Such an explanation would be utterly pointless if sprinkling was the mode used.

The theology of baptism in the New Testament requires immersion

The controlling idea in Christian baptism is union with Christ in his death and resurrection. This is clearly taught by Paul in Romans 6:3,4: 'Do you not know that as many of us who were baptized into Christ Jesus were baptized into His death? Therefore we were buried with Him through baptism into death, that just as Christ was raised from the dead by the glory of the Father, even so we also should walk in newness of life.' In other words, union with Christ crucified and risen signifies the believer's participation in the virtue of Christ's death and in the power of his resurrection; it signifies the end (by death and burial) of the old life of sin, and the beginning (by resurrection or rebirth) of a new life of righteousness. This is the primary meaning of baptism, and according to Conybeare and Howson, this passage 'cannot be understood without remembering that the primitive method of baptism was by immersion.'

You see, Christian baptism is designed to show forth very clearly that when a person becomes a Christian, two things happen. First, his old way of life ceases; and secondly, a completely new way of life begins. To quote Sanday and Headlam (also Anglicans, like Conybeare and Howson), 'When we descended into the baptismal water, that meant that we died with Christ to sin. When the water closed over our heads, that meant that we lay buried with him, in proof that our death to sin, like his death, was real' (*International Critical Commentary – Romans*). Likewise, just as Christ was raised from the dead by the power of God, so we are lifted from the waters of the baptismal pool to live a new and distinctive life of holiness in the power of his resurrection. A few drops of water sprinkled on a person's forehead or even a jug of water poured over their head, cannot by any stretch of imagination convey such a cardinal truth of salvation.

True, there are other images of baptism in the New Testament, but they all derive their efficacy and meaning from the main blessing of God's covenant of grace which is union with Christ in his death and resurrection. For example, baptism speaks of forgiveness of sin (Jer. 31:34; Ezek. 36:25; Matt. 26:28; Acts 2:38), and the washing away of the defilement of sin which estranges us from God (Acts 22:16; 1 Cor. 6:11; Titus 3:5). But this blessing is only ours because of Christ's baptism at Calvary (his immersion in the suffering of God-forsakenness on the cross, Luke 12:50) where he paid the penalty for sin once for all.

Baptism also speaks of new birth (John 3:3-7; Jer. 31:31-34; Ezek. 36:26-27) which is effected by the gift of baptism of the Holy Spirit (Matt. 3:11; John 3:8; Acts 2:38). But the gift of the Holy Spirit is only possible because of Christ's resurrection and ascension to heaven to receive the promise of the Spirit from the Father (Luke 24:48; Acts 1:6). Or to use the language of Paul, we who are dead in trespasses and sins can only be made alive spiritually if we are 'raised up with Christ' for 'God ... even when we were dead in trespasses, made us alive together with Christ (by grace you have been saved), and raised us up together ...' (Eph. 2:5-6).

Moreover, both images (our cleansing from sin and our resurrection to new life) are best conveyed by the symbol of immersion. Nothing can better display the power of Christ's death to wash away all sin, and the power of his resurrection to quicken sinners to new life, than the immersion and re-emergence of the believer from the water of the baptismal pool. Affusion could only be a suitable symbol of both these truths if the candidate were drenched under a waterfall or shower. But even then, it would merely portray the result of these blessings (the person's whole life being cleansed and brought into contact with the presence and power of the Holy Spirit). It could not convey the truth that the source and ground of these blessings are in the death and resurrection of Jesus Christ. So I am bold to say that only immersion does justice to all the theological images of baptism, and that is why it is the divinely ordained mode taught in Scripture.

The testimony of many theologians and historians supports immersion

It was not until the thirteenth century or so, that the practice of immersion was dropped in Western churches. The Greek and Russian Orthodox churches, however, still practise it. And even the Church of England Prayer Book states that infants are only to be sprinkled with water when they are certified too sickly to endure immersion. It would seem, however, as Spurgeon once caustically commented, that there is a large number of sickly babes at Anglican fonts!

Dante the 13th century poet mentions in his great poem, the 'Inferno', how he rescued a child from drowning in the baptistry of St. John, Florence.

Martin Luther wrote, 'I could wish that such as are to be baptized should be completely immersed into water, according to the meaning of the word and to the significance of the ordinance ... because it would be beautiful to have a full and perfect sign of so perfect a thing; as also without doubt it was instituted by Christ.'

Tyndale, the great English reformer, wrote of baptism, 'The plunging into the water signifieth that we die and are buried with Christ, as concerning the old life of sin, which is Adam; and the pulling out again signifieth that we rise again with Christ in a new life.'

Calvin, the greatest theologian amongst the Reformers, wrote, 'Whether the person baptized is to be wholly immersed ... or whether he is only to be sprinkled with water, is not of the least consequence: churches should be at liberty to adopt either ... although it is evident that the term baptize means to immerse, and that this was the form used by the primitive church' (*Institutes IV* chap.xv.19).

John Wesley, in a sermon on Romans 6:4 says, 'We are buried with him – alluding to the ancient manner of baptising by immersion.' It is also interesting that on May 5th, 1736, John Wesley refused to baptize a baby in Savannah save by dipping, because it was strong and healthy; and he was afterwards prosecuted for his refusal.

Dr. Schaff, in his *History of the Apostolic Church,* says, 'Respecting the form of baptism, the impartial historian is compelled by exegesis and history substantially to yield the point to the Baptists' (p.570).

Dean Stanley said, 'The change from immersion to sprinkling has set aside the larger part of the apostolic language regarding baptism, and has altered the very meaning of the word' (*Nineteenth Century*, Oct.1879).

Chapter Eight
The Meaning of Baptism

The best way to approach the meaning of baptism is to appreciate that baptism, like the Lord's Supper, is a sacrament – a sacred pledge and sign of what God has done for every truly penitent believer in Christ. It is therefore essentially a sacrament of grace, that is, a sacrament of divine initiative, not of human activity. The clearest evidence of this is the fact that in the New Testament the command is to 'be baptized' (Acts 2:38, passive imperative). Although the prophet Elisha told Naaman to dip himself in the river Jordan, Peter did not tell his hearers on the day of Pentecost to dip themselves, but rather to go and 'be baptized'. In other words, they were to get somebody else to immerse them. There is no command in the New Testament to anybody to baptize himself, and no instance of anyone doing it. The commands are exclusively to baptize others and to get others to baptize us, but never to baptize ourselves.

This is no insignificant detail, but an important part of the symbolism of baptism. For the fact that baptism is administered to us by someone else teaches us that salvation is by grace alone, something that is done for us and given to us by God. The minister who baptizes us, does so in a representative capacity. He stands for Jesus Christ, for it is Jesus Christ alone who bestows upon us the blessings of salvation.

It is for this reason that Peter in Acts 2:38 told the crowd to 'be baptized in the name of Jesus Christ.' In other passages the formula is 'into the name of the Lord Jesus,' (e.g. Acts 19:5) since baptism signifies union with Christ in his death and resurrection. But here the preposition is not 'into' but 'in', because Jesus Christ is the person on whose authority baptism is administered. To do something in somebody's name is to do it on his authority. Thus the minister does not presume to baptize people in his own name, but in the name of Jesus Christ as his representative.

Now, granted that baptism is a sacrament of grace, what does it signify? The answer to this question is threefold.

Baptism signifies union with Christ

God's chief grace to undeserving sinners is his plan to unite them to his Son. That this is the primary meaning of baptism is clear from the use of the preposition *eis* (into) with the verb 'to baptize.' Just as the passage of the Jews through the Red Sea was a baptism *eis* (into) Moses (1 Cor. 10:2), so Christian baptism is not into any man (1 Cor. 1:13) but into Christ (Rom. 6:3; Acts 8:16, 19:5).

It is true that, according to Matthew's account of the institution of baptism, baptism was to be into the one name of the three persons of the Trinity (Matt. 28:19), but this gives place in Acts and in the Epistles to baptism into the name of Jesus. This is because it is Jesus who revealed the Father and sent the Holy Spirit, and therefore we cannot be related to him without being related to them also.

Further, baptism into the name of Christ is baptism into Christ crucified and risen (Rom. 6:3,4; Col. 2:11-14). In 1 Corinthians 15:3,4 Paul gives a concise statement of the good news of salvation. 'I delivered to you first of all that which I also received: that Christ died for our sins according to the Scriptures, and that He was buried, and that He rose again the third day according to the Scriptures.' It is through the death, the burial and the resurrection of Jesus Christ that we receive God's gift of new life. We are saved through Christ, crucified and risen, but only if we are united with him in his death and resurrection. This union is entered into through faith and expressed and exhibited in baptism.

Thus, when confessing our faith in baptism, we are immersed in the water to declare the fact that we are united with Christ in his death. As we go down into the water, we are saying in effect that, as Jesus died for our sin on the cross, so we have died in him to sin in our lives. There has been a real and complete break with the past – a death resulting in burial. Indeed our baptism is a kind of funeral service and the water a grave whereby we are said to be 'buried with Him (Christ) in baptism' (Rom. 6:4). Death followed by burial now prevents our returning to our former way of life. And this is why Paul can ask the question, 'How can we who died (in our baptism) to sin, still live in it?' (Rom. 6:2).

But as Christ was raised from the dead by the mighty power of God, so we too, emerging from the baptismal waters, are raised with him into newness of life (Rom. 6:4,5). We are lifted from the water to live a new and distinctive life, the life of Christ himself. This life marks a radical break with our past, as Paul testifies: 'I have been crucified with Christ. It is no longer I who lives, but Christ who lives in me' (Gal. 2:20). The Christian life is not living up to an ideal; it is living out the new life we have received from Christ when he baptized us into his Spirit (Rom. 8:9-11). Day by day our baptism must spur us on to consider ourselves 'dead to sin and alive to God in Christ Jesus' (Rom. 6:11; see also Eph. 2:1-7).

The Christian life, therefore, is essentially a dying and rising life, and it is this to which baptism calls the penitent believer. It pledges my total loyalty to a Lord who bids me come and die. And it reminds me for the rest of my days that this calling involves dying continually to my sinful self and rising from that death to sin by the power of his indwelling Holy Spirit. So the Christian life may be rightly called the baptismal life, because it is all about dying and rising with Jesus who 'Himself bore our sins in His body on the tree, that we, having died to sins, might live for righteousness' (1 Peter 2:24).

There can be no doubt, then, that union with Christ in his death and resurrection is the chief blessing of God's salvation and the controlling idea of baptism. The next two meanings of baptism simply amplify the benefits of sharing in the death and resurrection of Christ.

Baptism signifies the forgiveness of sins

It is safe to say that all religious water rituals in the Old Testament were purification ceremonies, and Christian baptism is no exception. At its simplest, baptism is a purification rite 'for the remission of sins' (Acts 2:38). 'Arise and be baptized, and wash away your sins, calling on the name of the Lord', said Ananias to Paul (Acts 22:16). Similarly, it is almost certain that the phrases 'but you were washed' (1 Cor. 6:11) and 'the washing of regeneration' (Titus 3:5) are references to baptism. Not that baptism by itself brings remission of sins. It should be obvious that water administered to a body cannot remove guilt from a soul. Indeed, it is incredible that anybody should imagine that it could. No, in baptism the washing of our bodies with pure water (Heb. 10:22) signifies the washing of our soul (from the defilement of sin) that took place when we put our faith in Jesus Christ crucified and risen for us men and our salvation.

Baptism signifies the gift of the Spirit

All four evangelists record the fact that John the Baptist contrasted his own water-baptism with the Spirit-baptism which Jesus as the promised Messiah would administer. 'I baptize you with water ... He will baptize you with the Holy Spirit' (Matt. 3:11). In view of this contrast, we would expect that when Jesus Christ began to baptize with the Spirit, all baptism with water would cease. But the fact that water-baptism continued, by special command of the risen Christ, suggests that it is now intended to signify the very Spirit-baptism with which it had previously been contrasted.

The Lord Jesus, just before his ascension, quoted the words of John the Baptist to the disciples with approval and applied them to the coming of the Holy Spirit on the day of Pentecost. Luke records that 'He commanded them not to depart from Jerusalem, but to wait for the Promise of the Father, "which", he said, "you have heard from Me; for John truly baptized with water, but you shall be baptized with the Holy Spirit not many days from now"' (Acts 1:4-5). Thus when Peter says, 'Be baptized and you will receive the gift of the Holy Spirit' (Acts 2:38), he is bringing the two baptisms together and making the one a picture of the other. In other words, the baptism of water by which a person is raised from a watery grave, signifies the baptism of the Spirit by which people are 'made alive' or 'raised' from a spiritual grave of trespasses and sins (Eph. 2:5,6).

This, then, is the meaning of salvation as it is portrayed in baptism. Salvation is a big and noble word; we must not minimise its greatness. It is not only a negative remitting of sins, but also a positive giving of the Spirit. It is not only justification, but also regeneration. It is not only cleansing of past guilt, but also the powerful indwelling of the Spirit for future holiness. Both are the distinctive blessings of the new covenant which God promised through his prophets (Jer. 31:31-34; Ezek. 36:25-27; Matt. 26:28), and both are visibly and vividly portrayed in baptism.

Indeed, as we shall see in the next chapter, baptism is the rite which publicly initiates believers into the new covenant. It is the sign which marks them out as members of the new covenant, for it signifies as nothing else can their union with Jesus Christ who is the mediator of the new covenant and the bestower of its blessings.

To sum up, baptism signifies union with Christ in his death and resurrection, involving the end of the old life (through the forgiveness of sins), and the beginning of a new life (through the gift of the Spirit). Or, if you prefer, baptism signifies union with Christ bringing both justification (a once-for-all cleansing and acceptance) and regeneration (a new birth by the Spirit into a life of righteousness).

To these three meanings of baptism we must add that incorporation into Christ includes incorporation into the body of Christ, the church. Baptism is not a solitary thing, marking me out as a Christian on my own. It is a corporate act, making us part of the body of Christ, with all the privileges, partnership and responsibility which that entails. (This will be more fully explored in chapter 10).

Chapter Nine
The Purpose of Baptism

We turn now from the meaning of baptism to its purpose; from what it signifies to what it does. In the previous chapter we sought to define the inward and spiritual grace of which baptism is the outward and visible sign. We must now go on to define the relation between the visible sacrament and the invisible grace, between the sign and the thing signified.

What baptism does not do

At the outset we must dismiss as erroneous the belief that baptism by itself automatically conveys the grace of salvation, so that all those who receive the sign automatically also receive the thing signified. The consequence of this view is to regard all baptized persons (especially infants) as regenerate. Or, conversely, it is to suppose that all persons who have not been baptized are therefore not saved.

Apart from the pragmatic argument that not all baptized persons seem to be regenerate, for they do not supply evidence of their regeneration in a life of godliness and holiness, there are two strong biblical arguments against this view. They concern the nature of the church and the way of salvation.

(1) The nature of the church

However unfashionable it may be today, the Bible does envisage a difference between the visible and the invisible church. We do not mean by this that a person can belong to the invisible church without responsible membership of a local Christian congregation. Rather, we mean that it is possible to belong to a local visible church without belonging to the true church, the body of Christ, which is invisible in the sense that its members are known to God alone. The apostle Paul recognises this possibility when he writes that 'The solid foundation of God stands, having this seal: "The Lord knows those who are His"' (2 Tim. 2:19). As Augustine wrote, 'Many of those within are without; and some of those without are within.' He was echoing John, of course, who says, of certain heretics that 'they went out from us, but they were not of us ...' (1 John 2:19). They were members (doubtless baptized members) but though 'with us' outwardly and visibly, they were not 'of us' (not genuine, but spurious).

Similarly, Paul writes at the beginning of 1 Corinthians 10 of the Old Testament church in the wilderness 'that our fathers were all baptized into Moses in the cloud and in the sea, and all ate the same spiritual food and all drank the same spiritual drink ... but with most of them God was not well pleased; for their bodies were scattered in the wilderness,' (verses 1-5). The apostle deliberately describes them as baptized communicants, who nevertheless were overthrown in the wilderness. He thus shows that we may be baptized and partake of the Lord's Supper and yet not be saved.

Now the significance of this very important distinction between the visible and invisible church is that the visible church consists of those who have been baptized while the invisible church consists of the regenerate. Since the two companies are not identical, not all who have been baptized are regenerate.

Simon Magus is an example. He professed faith, was baptized, and no doubt passed as a church member. But Peter described him as being 'poisoned by bitterness and bound by iniquity', with his 'heart not right in the sight of God' (Acts 8:13-23).

The words of Paul about circumcision are just as applicable to baptism. 'For he is not a real Jew who is one outwardly, nor is circumcision that which is outward in the flesh; but he is a Jew who is one inwardly; and circumcision is that of the heart, in the spirit, not in the letter' (Rom. 2:28,29).

(2) The way of salvation

The other strong argument against baptismal regeneration is the fact that over and over again the New Testament writers declare that we are justified or saved by grace through faith. Paul declares 'We ... know that a man is not justified by the works of the law, but by faith in Jesus Christ' (Gal. 2:16). And again in Galatians 3:26: 'For you are all sons of God through faith in Christ Jesus.' Finally in Ephesians 2:8 he states: 'For by grace you have been saved through faith, and that not of yourselves; it is the gift of God, not of works, lest anyone should boast.' It is impossible to reconcile this apostolic doctrine with the heretical view that justification is by grace through baptism, with or without faith.

Now it is true that in 1 Peter 3:21 the apostle says that 'baptism now saves you' (literal translation), but the context clearly shows that he is referring to baptism as a picture of our salvation and not the means of our salvation. For he likens our salvation to the salvation of Noah and his family in the ark during the destruction of the world by the flood. Indeed, he speaks of baptism as 'the like figure' (literally the anti-type) or fulfilment of the salvation of the human race foreshadowed in Noah and the flood. The connection, of course, is that these two things have a common element, namely, water as an instrument of death. The flood was the judgement of God on a sinful world in which the majority of the human race was destroyed.

But unlike them, when Christ took the judgement of God that our sins justly deserved and died in our place, he rose again on the third day to save us. And in doing so, he lifted us, like the ark, above the sure destruction of God's judgement. Just as Noah and his family were saved through being in the ark, so we are saved through being 'in Christ', not through the waters of baptism. And to make sure he is not misunderstood, Peter says that baptism saves us, not by 'the removal of the filth of the flesh, but (as) the answer of a good conscience towards God through the resurrection of Jesus Christ.'

It is not the water of baptism that cleanses us, for then only our flesh would be clean. It is our conscience that is defiled and the water of baptism can't reach that. What then is the purpose of baptism? Peter replies that it is 'the answer of a good conscience toward God.' Baptism is the outward confession of our faith in Christ as the one whose death and resurrection are enough to save our soul and give us a 'good conscience' in place of the evil one we have always had.

An outward, bodily operation cannot secure the salvation of the soul or be an indispensable condition of salvation. What Paul writes in Romans 6 about being baptized into Christ must not be interpreted in such a way that it contradicts his teaching in chapters three to five of the same epistle, namely that we are justified by faith alone. No, the New Testament is quite clear:

a man cannot be saved through baptism without faith (Mark 16:16), nor is he condemned because he believes but has not been baptized. The thief on the cross believed and went to heaven without being baptized (Luke 23:42,43), and Cornelius received the Holy Spirit (was regenerated) before he was baptized (Acts 10:44-48).

What baptism does

Christian baptism as the initiatory rite of God's new covenant with men, may be said to do three things –

(1) It publicly declares our faith in Christ

Faith in essence is an invisible, intangible thing which needs to be expressed in action. It is a personal encounter with God in which our spirit surrenders to the control and possession of Christ's Spirit. It takes place in the deepest recesses of our being and as such it is a secret experience. But in baptism we show people what they cannot see; we declare what they may not have already guessed, that our faith is in Jesus Christ.

Thus baptism is a mark by which a Christian may be distinguished from a non-Christian. Just as a wedding ring is a mark of difference by which a married woman is distinguished from one who is unmarried, so baptism marks out a Christian from a non-Christian. It is the Christian's identity card. This is specially the case in countries where the church is a persecuted minority. Once a person has been baptized, he is publicly recognised as a Christian. Perhaps he has been a secret believer for some time, but baptism is the decisive and irrevocable step, the crossing of the boundary into open discipleship.

Baptism makes him a marked man. It may expose him to persecution, disinheritance and even death. But even in so-called Christian countries, there is always a price to pay in following Christ, but the reward outweighs the cost.

Baptism, then, is a public confession of a private, personal faith in Jesus Christ. It is a way of coming out into the open and nailing our colours to the mast. It is, to quote Paul, the making of 'the good confession in the presence of many witnesses' (1 Tim. 6:12). So however difficult it may be for us to confess our faith in Christ through baptism, we should never be afraid or ashamed to do so.

> Ashamed of Jesus! – sooner far
> Let evening blush to own a star;
> He sheds the beams of light divine
> O'er this benighted soul of mine.
>
> Ashamed of Jesus! that dear Friend
> On whom my hopes of heaven depend!
> No; when I blush, be this my shame,
> That I no more revere His name.
>
> *Joseph Grigg (c. 1720 – 68)*

Paul said, 'I am not ashamed of the gospel' (Romans 1:16). Let us be equally glad to confess that our lives belong to Jesus Christ. For Jesus said, 'Whoever confesses Me before men, him will I also confess before My Father who is in heaven; but whoever denies Me before men, him I will also deny before My Father who is in heaven' (Matt. 10:32,33).

(2) It solemnly commits our life to Christ

When we are converted we promise to follow Jesus Christ, and we offer our lives for his service. In baptism this promise is solemnly and publicly sealed. It is a going over in ink what you have already written in pencil. And it is this use of baptism which lies behind the term 'sacrament' as applied to baptism and the Lord's Supper. They are religious rites which Jesus gave to his disciples by means of which they could swear their allegiance to him.

The term sacrament, as we have already seen, comes from the Latin word *sacramentum.* It referred to the military oath which was repeated by a soldier when he joined a Roman legion, his hands being placed between those of his commander. It was something the soldier did when enlisting. And in this way he solemnly committed himself to a life of loyalty and dedicated service to the Emperor.

In the same way baptism is the *sacramentum,* the vow of allegiance, of the Christian soldier. It is your promise to be Christ's faithful soldier and servant to the end of your life. And it is a step which must not be taken lightly. We must be true to our vow. It will mean leaving behind the things that grieve Jesus Christ and giving ourselves wholly and unconditionally to him. 'No one engaged in warfare entangles himself with the affairs of this life, that he may please him who enlisted him as a soldier' (2 Tim. 2:4).

> In full and glad surrender
> I give myself to thee,
> Thine utterly and only
> And evermore to be.

Frances Ridley Havergal (1836 –79)

It would be a serious thing for a Roman soldier to go back on his oath and desert the ranks. It is a very sad thing when a husband or wife break their marriage vows. But it is an even greater tragedy when a Christian goes back to his old sinful way of life. Let us determine, God helping us, never to turn back. Jesus Christ said, 'No one, having put his hand to the plough and looking back, is fit for the kingdom of God' (Luke 9:62). Satan will contest our dedication to Jesus Christ all the way by fierce temptation, bitter disappointment and even persecution. But in all these trials we are never alone. The Lord Jesus will stand by us and strengthen us (2 Tim. 4:17).

(3) It visibly seals God's promises to us in Christ

Because fallen man does not always keep his word, he finds it hard, if not impossible, to believe that other people will keep theirs. So for reassurance, men from the earliest times, have sought to have, in addition to the bare words of another person, some solemn sign or visible pledge to act as a guarantee that the promise will be fulfilled. 'I love you and will be true to you for ever,' says a bridegroom to his bride, and gives her a ring. Confirming solemn promises by visible, tangible tokens is an important thing in the world. And if what is promised is highly prized, receiving and possessing the token will bring delight and assurance.

Ask a bride how she feels when her bridegroom slips on the wedding ring as his pledge of lifelong fidelity! Ask a happily married woman what thoughts a glance at her wedding ring conjure up! So, too, baptism is the heavenly Bridegroom's token of commitment pledging endless care and joy to the believer. And receiving and reflecting on baptism is meant to bring us joy and assurance. God has not just given us a 'naked' word to believe. He has 'clothed' his promises of grace. He has made them visible and tangible in the sacraments so that our poor, weak faith may be strengthened.

This is the Godward side of the sacraments and Paul saw such a meaning in circumcision. In Romans 4:11 Abraham is said to have 'received the sign of circumcision, a seal of the righteousness of the faith which he had while still uncircumcised.' Here it is said that Abraham received two gifts. First, he received justification (a righteous relationship with God) by faith, while still uncircumcised. Secondly, he received circumcision as a sign and seal of this righteousness. The righteousness was given him in Genesis 15; its seal was received in Genesis 17 (more than 13 years later, see Gen. 16:16).

Now what circumcision was to Abraham, baptism is to us. It is not only the sign of covenant membership, but a seal or pledge of covenant blessings. Baptism does not convey these blessings to us, but conveys to us a right or title to them, so that if we truly believe, we inherit the blessings which baptism 'estates' upon us, as the Reformers used to say. The blessings which are pictured, proclaimed and promised in baptism are not bestowed unconditionally; they are appropriated by faith. For as the seal of God's covenant, baptism is like a will (the Greek word *diathēkē* can mean either a 'last will and testament' or a 'covenant') which may be said to convey to us a fortune, but which does nothing of the sort if we do not claim it.

The writer of the letter to the Hebrews emphasises the costly grace of God in the restoring of the new covenant: 'And for this reason He is the Mediator of the new covenant, by means of death, for the redemption of the transgressions under the first covenant, that those who are called may receive the promise of the eternal inheritance. For where there is a testament, there must also of necessity be the death of the testator. For a testament is in force after men are dead, since it has no power at all while the testator lives. Therefore not even the first covenant was dedicated without blood' (Heb. 9:15-18).

Thus Paul says, 'In baptism ... you also were raised with Him through faith' (Col. 2:12). A right and worthy reception of the sacraments is a believing reception. Since a sacrament is a 'visible word' (Augustine), and it is the function of God's Word to arouse faith (Rom. 10:17), the sacraments stimulate our faith to lay hold of the blessings which they signify and seal to us. An unworthy reception of the sacraments brings not blessing, but judgement according to Paul: 'Therefore whoever eats this bread or drinks this cup of the Lord in an unworthy manner will be guilty of the body and blood of the Lord. But let a man examine himself, and so let him eat of the bread and drink of the cup. For he who eats and drinks in an unworthy manner eats and drinks judgement to himself, not discerning the Lord's body.' (1 Cor. 11:27-29).

The question may be asked, if baptism does not by itself confer the graces it signifies (but only a title to them), why does the Bible sometimes speak as if it does? For example, baptism 'now saves us' (1 Peter 3:21), or 'Arise and be baptized, and wash away your sins' (Acts 22:16). The answer, quite simply, is that the Bible never envisages the baptism of an unbeliever. In the first quotation Peter says that 'baptism is the answer (or believing response) of a good conscience toward God through the resurrection of Jesus Christ.' And in the second Ananias tells Paul to 'wash away your sins, calling on the name of the Lord' (which is, of course, an act of faith). And since 'baptism and faith are but the outside and the inside of the same thing' (James Denney), the Bible can ascribe to baptism the blessings of the new covenant that really belong to faith.

You can see, then, what a dangerously mistaken doctrine it is which says that it is baptism which saves the sinner and washes away his sins. Baptism is only a sign and seal of God's covenant of salvation with believing sinners. And as such, it calls forth faith not in itself, but in its author and in his word. Baptism, therefore, is God's personal pledge to the believer of what he has already received by faith. In it God's promises to him of forgiveness and new life are visibly signed and sealed. His faith is further aroused and strengthened. And his assurance of salvation is increased.

This is what baptism does, according to the New Testament. And it would be wrong either to invest it with magical powers it does not have, or to devalue a means of grace that stimulates and strengthens. Martin Luther, who rediscovered the blessings of justification by faith for the church, was often beset by the most frightening temptations. But in those moments of despair, he buoyed his soul by saying to himself, *'baptizatus sum'* (I have been baptized). Thus he regained assurance that God's gracious call to him was sure, and that he must not waver in responding to it. He understood the purpose of baptism! Do we?

Chapter Ten
The Outcome of Baptism

Being baptized is not an end in itself. Commitment to a local congregation of believers in whose fellowship you are to grow spiritually is the end to which baptism leads. The New Testament never divorces a Christian profession from church membership. In fact, conversion is described as 'the Lord adding to the church' (Acts 2:47). In the mind of Paul to be 'baptized into Christ' (Gal. 3:27) is to be 'baptized into one body' (1 Cor. 12:13).

When we are born again, we are not born in an isolation hospital! We are born into God's family, the church. Discipleship and church-manship belong together like love and marriage. The New Testament never envisages a Christian who is not a church member. Those who came to know Christ committed themselves at once to a local church where they were instructed and cared for. So on the day of Pentecost 'those who gladly received his word were baptized; and that day about three thousand souls were added to them. And they continued steadfastly in the apostles' doctrine and fellowship, in the breaking of bread, and in prayers' (Acts 2:41-42).

Although the Christian life is intensely personal, it is not meant to be solitary. We are not to live our Christian lives in selfish isolation. That is not Christianity. The Christian life is essentially communal and corporate. God's purpose is not just to save independent souls, but to build a church, to create a community of true believers who are as committed to each other as they are to him. It is in church fellowship that believers 'grow up' into Christ the head of the church, 'joined and knit together by what every joint supplies, according to the effective working by which every part does its share' (Eph. 4:15-16).

Thus the New Testament describes the church as a family in which we are all brothers and sisters, as a kingdom in which we are fellow-citizens, and as the body of Christ of which he is the head, and we the members. We are to be together like sheep in the same flock under the same shepherd, like branches of the vine, like stones built together to make the temple of God. In other words, we are to belong to each other as we belong to him.

Baptism the doorway into church membership

In the New Testament the doorway into the fellowship of a local congregation of Christians was baptism. By it a person separated himself from the world and joined himself to the church. Take the day of Pentecost as a case in point. Peter's final appeal to his hearers was, 'Be saved from this perverse generation.' In other words, come out from among the sinners you are at present standing with and join us. And Luke says, 'Then those who gladly received his word were baptized, and that day about three thousand souls were added to them' (Acts 2:40-41).

By their baptism these new converts separated themselves from the Israel that had rejected Christ, to join the new Israel that owned his salvation and sovereignty. And they committed themselves to meet regularly for teaching, fellowship, prayers, breaking of bread and contributing to one another's needs. Luke says that 'they continued steadfastly in the apostles' doctrine and fellowship, in the breaking of bread, and in prayers. Then fear came upon every soul, and many wonders and signs were done through the apostles. Now all who believed were together, and had all things in common, and sold their possessions and goods, and divided them among all, as anyone had need. So continuing daily with one accord in the temple, and breaking bread from house to house, they ate their food with gladness and simplicity of heart, praising God and having favour with all the people. And the Lord added to the church daily those who were being saved.' (Acts 2:42-47).

Today, unfortunately, in some churches baptism and church membership are treated as separate issues. People feel that as long as they belong to the invisible, universal church, that is all that matters. But this is quite wrong. The apostles believed and taught that the invisible church must be expressed through the visible church on earth. They saw each local congregation as a visible manifestation of the one true church. The term 'the church' and the term 'the body of Christ' are applied in the New Testament both to the local visible congregation and the invisible universal church. The one is as much 'the church' as the other. So Paul writes 'To the church of God which is at Corinth (i.e. local church 1 Cor. 1:21), and that 'God gave the Lord Jesus to be head over all things the church' (i.e. the universal church, Eph. 1:22).

It is therefore quite wrong to suppose that you can belong to the universal, invisible church without belonging to its local, visible counterpart in the place where you live. The New Testament never considers the possibility of a believer living his Christian life outside the context of the local church. Membership of the invisible church should automatically express itself in membership of some local visible church.

Here, then, is the double confession of baptism as far as church membership is concerned. It is an opportunity to declare yourself a Christian and to be declared a Christian. In his baptism a person confesses that he is a Christian and asks to be acknowledged as such. He wants to be identified with his fellow-believers as a follower of Christ. In baptising him, the members of the church signify their wholehearted acceptance of his profession of Christianity and receive him into their fellowship. Thus it is only after a person is baptized that he is allowed to break bread with that particular group of believers and come under the care and control of the elders.

To sum up, by the Spirit we are baptized into the invisible church, the church as God sees it. By water we are baptized into the visible church, the church as man sees it. No one should be baptized who is not also prepared to become a church member. And no one should be received into membership who is not willing publicly to declare their faith in Christ by baptism.

The importance of continuing in the faith

Post-baptism listlessness is a common malady; be on your guard against it. When your baptism is behind you and you have been received into church membership, it is no time to sit back and rest on your oars. It is time rather to press ahead with vigour and determination. While in Antioch, Paul and Barnabas spoke to the converts and 'persuaded them to continue in the grace of God' (Acts 13:43). They returned later, 'strengthening the souls of the disciples, exhorting them to continue in the faith, and saying, "We must through many tribulations enter the kingdom of God"' (Acts 14:22).

Now there are four things we must devote ourselves to if we are to go on in our Christian life, rather than go back. You will find all four mentioned in Acts 2:41-42, 'So those who gladly received his word were baptized ... and they continued steadfastly in the apostles' doctrine and fellowship, in the breaking of bread, and in the prayers.'

(1) 'The apostles' teaching'

Jesus sent the disciples into the world to preach the gospel and to baptize those who would believe. He also added to the great commission these words, 'teaching them to observe all things that I have commanded you' (Matt. 28:20). Our Lord had spent three years teaching his disciples before sending them into the world to teach others. And the truths they taught their converts by word of mouth are written down for us in the New Testament. If, therefore, we are to devote ourselves to the apostles' teaching, it will be necessary for us to set aside time each day for the thoughtful study of the New Testament, and indeed the whole Bible.

The Bible is food for the soul because it is the Word of God. Our Lord affirmed that 'Man shall not live by bread alone, but by every word that proceeds from the mouth of God' (Matthew 4:4). Peter underlines how essential God's Word is: 'As new-born babes, desire the pure milk of the word, that you may grow thereby' (1 Peter 2:2). The Christian will fall ill if he neglects it and starve if he ignores it altogether. So read the Bible first thing in the morning and last thing at night, and persevere in it until it becomes a habit that nothing but illness can break. Use a good modern translation like the New King James Version or the New International Version which are easier to understand than the old King James Version. Obtain reliable

Bible notes that will supply you with graded explanatory notes to suit your age and spiritual experience. If in the morning you read the passage set by the Bible notes, in the evening you can work your way through the New Testament, or vice versa. But please read your Bible prayerfully, and not just as you would read the newspaper. As you open the Word of God, humble yourself before him and pray, 'Open my eyes, that I may see wondrous things from Your law' (Ps. 119:18). By ourselves we cannot understand all that we read; we need the illumination of the Holy Spirit to discern it and apply it faithfully to our lives (1 Cor. 2:14).

It will be necessary, however, not only to read the Bible quietly by yourself at home, but also to study it regularly with others in Bible classes and worship services where the meaning of God's Word is faithfully explained. Only in this way can we build up our faith and discover God's will for our lives. All we need for daily living is contained in the Bible. As someone has said, 'It contains light to direct you, food to support you, comfort to cheer you and armour to protect you. It is the traveller's map, the pilgrim's staff, the pilot's compass, the soldier's sword and the Christian's charter.'

To devote ourselves to the apostles' doctrine or teaching is to steep and saturate our minds in the Word of God. Paul said to Timothy, 'Continue in what you have learned and been assured of' (2 Tim. 3:14). And our Lord said, 'If you abide in My word, you are My disciples indeed. And you shall know the truth, and the truth shall set you free' (John 8:31).

(2) 'Fellowship'

Christian fellowship refers to the close and intimate relationship believers share both with Jesus Christ and with one another. The early Christians thrived on this deep sense of friendship as they worshipped together, prayed together and enjoyed Christ together. No Christian was ever meant to go it alone. We need to spend time with Jesus Christ and with others of like mind. 'Birds of a feather flock together.' Christians need to keep together or the pressures of the world and the opposition of Satan will weaken our faith.

This means every Christian needs to belong to a company of believers where God's Word is faithfully preached, and meet weekly with his fellow-believers to glorify God. 'Let us consider one another in order to stir up love and good works, not forsaking the assembling of ourselves together as is the manner of some' (Heb. 10:24-25). If we stay away from Christian fellowship, our love for the Lord Jesus will soon cool off just as a piece of coal taken out of the fire and placed on the hearth soon becomes cold and dead. To be in the company of real Christians is like being in the centre of a fire, because when we are together with Jesus Christ in our midst, he kindles a fire of love in our hearts which generates warm and spiritual fellowship that is mutually enriching.

It is, of course, a great privilege to be a member of a local church, but it carries with it the responsibility of doing all we can to contribute to the ministry of that church in worship and witness. It will demand time, effort and money if it is going to be maintained and increased. We will also have to be careful not to spoil the fellowship by unkind or selfish actions. Satan loves to break down and ruin the effectiveness of Christian fellowship.

(3) 'Breaking of bread'

The chief expression of worship for Christians is the Lord's

Supper. It is the central service of the church, and it was instituted by the Lord Jesus himself. 'He took bread, gave thanks and broke it, and gave it to them, saying, "This is My body which is given for you; do this in remembrance of Me."' (Luke 22:19). He knew just how forgetful we can be and how prone to stray from him, so he gave us this simple object lesson. It reminds us continually of the great price he paid to free us from sin. The bread signifies his body broken on the cross, whereas the poured out wine symbolises his blood shed for the forgiveness of our sins. Both are intended 'to proclaim the Lord's death till He comes' (1Cor. 11:26). The words, 'do this' are in the present continuous tense, which means that we are to keep on observing the Lord's Supper until his return when we will drink of the fruit of the vine in his Father's kingdom (Matt. 26:29).

So if we have obeyed Christ's command to be baptized, we must also obey his demand to break bread in remembrance of him. The early Christians met every Sunday to do so: 'On the first day of the week, the disciples came together to break bread.' (Acts 20:7). The Lord's Day was inconceivable without the Lord's Supper. To neglect attendance at the Lord's Table is to deprive ourselves of a special means of grace, because in this feast our Lord comes to us afresh in forgiveness and love to draw us closer to himself and to renew us for his service. Our eyes see the symbols; but our faith (of which eating and drinking are the perfect physical equivalents) looks beyond the symbols to the reality for which they stand, and thankfully appropriates anew the saving benefits of Christ's precious body and blood.

As in baptism, the blessing is not in the elements themselves, but in our believing response to them. To quote from one of Spurgeon's sermons on the Lord's Supper, 'We not only eat of his bread, but symbolically we feast upon him … I believe in the real presence of Christ: I do not believe in the carnal presence of the Romanist. I believe in the *real* presence to the believer; but that reality is none the less real because it is spiritual.'

There are other means of grace, as we have seen, such as the teaching of God's Word and the fellowship of his people. The Lord's Supper is yet another. Do not neglect it. It is a most blessed and enriching experience to gather again and again around the Lord's Table with the Lord's people to remember his death and have our faith strengthened and our love for him nourished.

(4) 'Prayers'

Those who believed and were baptized 'continued steadfastly in … prayers'. This is the fourth means of grace mentioned in Acts 2:42. The Christian life is a life of prayer, in that it is a life of communion with God through Christ. Prayer, in the words of a well-known hymn,

> 'is the Christian's vital breath,
> the Christian's native air.'

> *James Montgomery (1771 – 1854)*

Without it there can be no growth or blessing. Private prayer is vital to the spiritual life of the individual while corporate prayer is essential for the spiritual prosperity of the church.

Our Lord certainly expected us to give ourselves to private prayer. He said, 'When you pray, go into your room, and when you have shut your door, pray to your Father who is in the secret place; and your Father who sees in secret will reward you openly' (Matt. 6:6). Indeed, our Lord himself is our supreme example. In Mark 1:35 we read, 'In the morning, having arisen a long while before day light, He went out and departed to a solitary place; and there He prayed.' If Jesus found it necessary to pray on his own to God, how much more should we!

Be as natural as possible. God is your heavenly Father. He wants you to talk to him about everything. Tell him how much you think of him, and what he means to you, and how greatly you love him. Confess your sins to him and tell him you are truly sorry. Thank him for all the things he has done for you. And then ask him for his help in all your needs. To make steady progress in the Christian life, it is very important to have a personal, daily 'quiet-time' with God. Guard this time jealously, for the devil will steal it from you if you are not careful and disciplined.

But prayer is just as important for the life of the whole church, because it is by public prayer that we seek God's direction for the congregation and the blessing of his Spirit on its worship and witness. At least two or three prayer meetings should be convened weekly at times to suit the members, and every member should try to attend one of those meetings. Too many, I am afraid, neglect the prayer meeting, and so rob themselves and the church of blessing and growth. They have not because they ask not (James 4:2).

The early Christians were great believers in praying together. 'When they had prayed, the place where they were assembled together was shaken; and they were all filled with the Holy Spirit, and they spoke the word of God with boldness' (Acts 4:31). And again, when 'many were gathered together praying', Peter was delivered from prison (Acts 12:12). Paul often solicited the prayers of the churches he visited, for example, 'Brethren, pray for us, that the word of the Lord may run swiftly and triumph, just as it is with you, and that we may be delivered from unreasonable and wicked men; for not all have faith' (2 Thess. 3:1-2). When God's people pray, the preaching of God's Word prevails. We owe it to ourselves and to the whole church at home and abroad to 'continue earnestly in prayer' (Col. 4:2). So let us give ourselves to a life of prayer like Samuel who said, 'Far be it from me that I should sin against the LORD in ceasing to pray for you' (1 Sam. 12:23).

This is what baptism leads on to. To quote Sir Winston Churchill's memorable words after the first great victory of the Second World War at El Alamein: 'This is not the end. It is not even the beginning of the end. But it is perhaps the end of the beginning.' The Christian life begins in earnest *after* baptism. And if we continue steadfastly in these things (the apostles' doctrine and fellowship, the breaking of bread and prayers) we shall see in our lives and in the church the blessed results of Acts 2:47. Our hearts will overflow with praise to God. We will have favour with all the people. And the Lord will add to our number day by day those who are being saved. What greater results could possibly flow from our baptism?

Chapter Eleven
One Baptism Once

More and more people are asking for re-baptism, even though they were baptized by immersion on profession of faith in Jesus Christ as their Lord and Saviour. On a trip to Israel, several Baptists and Pentecostalists in our party were re-baptized because they wanted to be able to say that they had been baptized in the River Jordan. I understand that this is a frequent occurrence.

According to a survey conducted by the Southern Baptist Convention's Home Mission Board (USA) in 1994, six of every ten adults baptized in Southern Baptist churches have been previously baptized by immersion on profession of faith. More than forty percent said that their second baptism was the result of rededication to Christ (*Religious Herald*, Virginia, April 13, 1995). Most pastors have similar requests from time to time, and many see no reason to deny re-baptism. Their justification for doing so is that baptism is not valid if it has not been preceded by a genuine conversion. It is a serious question for all concerned to do some rethinking.

The contradiction of re-baptism

Re-baptism destroys the very meaning of the sacrament our

Lord ordained. For baptism speaks of the new birth (John 3:5). It is an initiation ceremony proclaiming the beginning of an altogether new life which will grow and develop like a baby maturing into an adult. And, like a birth, baptism is both necessary and unrepeatable. It is by definition impossible to have more than one spiritual birth, and therefore unthinkable to have more than one rite of initiation.

Again, baptism speaks of acquittal and forgiveness (Acts 2:38; Romans 8:1,33). It is a ceremony of washing, declaring that the charge-sheet against us has been wiped clean so that there is no record of any wrongdoing against us. Baptism is the sacrament of justification by the sheer grace of God, and it is once for all. You can no more be re-baptized than you can be re-justified.

And then, too, baptism speaks of union with Christ (Galatians 3:26,27; Romans 6:3,4). The phrase 'baptized into Christ' or 'into the name of Christ' means incorporation into the life and ownership of the one named. It is a wedding ceremony in which I am publicly 'betrothed' to Jesus my Lord in a covenant relationship, 'for better for worse', not just till I die, but for ever. And like a wedding, baptism cannot be done again. Sometimes people get married even though they do not love the other partner. Should they fall in love with that person at a later stage, there is no need for another marriage service.

Re-baptism is a travesty because it makes nonsense of the gospel of Jesus Christ. It sacrifices the objectivity of God's grace on the altar of human subjectivity. It calls the verities of salvation mentioned above into question and makes God a liar. How can the on-looking world take the claims of baptism seriously if we affirm them one moment and deny them the next?

The components of a valid baptism

(1) A personal profession of faith in Jesus Christ

Baptism is a twofold act of witness. It is first and foremost a witness to the grace of God uniting me with Christ in his death and resurrection and making me a member of his kingdom. But it is also a confession of my personal response to the grace of God; my own profession of repentance from sin and faith in Christ. Thus the minister asks the candidate both privately before the service and publicly during the service whether he has truly repented of his sin and put his trust personally in Jesus Christ crucified and risen as his Lord and Saviour.

If the person replies in the affirmative and gives credible evidence before the church of living a Christian life, he should be baptized. We have no means or mandate to go further than that. Only God can read a person's heart and know their true motives. 1 Samuel 16:7, 'Man looks at the outward appearance, but the LORD looks at the heart.' So their profession of faith has to be accepted at face value, as was Simon's (Acts 8:13-24).

If, however, they later discover that they were mistaken in their belief that they were Christians; or if they professed faith simply to please a spouse or their parents, it would not be right for the church to re-baptize them. For one thing, the Bible does not sanction re-baptism. And for another, how can the church be sure they are sincere or have enough faith this time?

A baptism personally requested on profession of faith in Christ is still a baptism, even if it is unaccompanied by an experience of God's grace.[1] It is like a marriage that has been contracted but not consummated. Without consummation the marriage could be declared null and void. But what is needed is not for the couple to go through the ceremony all over again, but to supply the missing part, physical consummation!

Philip's ministry at Samaria is a case in point (Acts 8:1-17). The Samaritans 'believed Philip as he preached good news about the kingdom of God and the name of Jesus Christ' (verse 12) and were baptized. But their faith and their baptism for some reason were not accompanied by the gift of the Holy Spirit, and so they were not yet saved or regenerated. It seems that God withheld the Spirit from them in order to get the apostles on the scene to approve the acceptance of half-caste Jews into the church (a departure from normal practice). Peter and John were accordingly sent to Samaria and 'they laid hands on them, and they received the Holy Spirit' (verse 17). What they did not do was to re-baptise them. They saw no need to repeat what had already been done. For there is but 'one Lord, one faith, one baptism' (Eph. 4:5). Christian baptism is unrepeatable!

Now the same cannot be said of infant baptism, because it cannot be regarded as a true baptism. A baptism which is administered to people without their consent or understanding of what they are doing is as much a travesty of the sacrament as re-baptism. It surely has no more claim to validity than the equally unacceptable practice of infant marriages. Such personal and life-affecting choices cannot be taken by parents on behalf of their infants, even though they are convinced they are acting in the child's best interests. A baptism is only valid if the candidate is immersed in water in the name of the Father, the Son and the Holy Spirit upon a personal and credible profession of faith in Jesus Christ as Saviour and Lord. Infant baptism is invalid not because the infant does not have enough faith, but because he has no faith at all.

This was the difference between the disciples at Ephesus (Acts 19:1-7) and the disciples at Samaria. The disciples at

Ephesus had received John's baptism, administered on the grounds of repentance. But it was devoid of faith as well as of an experience of regeneration! In fact, they told Paul they did not know that Christ had come or that they could receive the Holy Spirit: 'When they heard this, they were baptized in the name of the Lord Jesus. And when Paul had laid his hands upon them, the Holy Spirit came on them' (verses 5-6).

This was not a re-baptism! What they received from Paul was the 'one baptism' of authentic Christianity. Their previous immersion in water was not the gospel ordinance, because without any knowledge of the gospel they were unable to profess their belief in the gospel. In this they were like infants. They were unable to believe because they had no knowledge of the gospel on which to base their belief. If that is your situation (if you were baptized as an infant or as a member of a cult such as the Mormons or Jehovah's Witnesses), you, too, need to receive the one, true baptism of the gospel. The other component of a valid baptism is –

(2) Immersion in water in the name of the Father, Son and Holy Spirit

We have already seen that the word baptize can only mean to dip or immerse. Matthew 28:19 says literally, 'Go therefore and make disciples of all the nations, immersing them in the name of the Father and of the Son and of the Holy Spirit.' It is only the continued reluctance of translators to translate the Greek word *baptizō* that allows the confusion to persist. One, therefore, can no more accept sprinkling for immersion than one could accept a 'yield' sign for a 'stop' sign. The one cannot do what the other can.

The mode of baptism is important if baptism is to be the

sign and seal of God's grace that our Lord intended it to be. True, sprinkling can also be a sign of cleansing. In the Old Testament the blood of animal sacrifices was sprinkled on the people to indicate that the life forfeited by the innocent victim was the only ground on which God could forgive their sin (Hebrews 9:13). But in the New Testament washing is the predominant symbol. 'Let us draw near ... having our hearts sprinkled from an evil conscience and our bodies washed with pure water' (Heb.10:22; see also Acts 22:16; 1 Cor. 6:11; Titus 3:5; Rev. 1:5, 7:14, 22;14).

Thus our Lord chose immersion rather than sprinkling as a better symbol of the power of his blood to wash away sin. Sprinkling gives a picture only of partial cleansing to the candidate and the onlooker. Nothing can replace immersion as a sign of the total cleansing of the believer by the blood of Christ's cross.

Moreover, he chose immersion because, unlike sprinkling or affusion, it alone can contain all the images of our salvation through the grace of God. Whether it be the washing away of sin, or the baptism of the Holy Spirit resulting in a new birth and a new life, or union with Christ in his death and resurrection, or deliverance from God's judgement of the world (like Noah at the flood, 1 Peter 3:20f), or the putting on of Christ (Gal. 3:27, we emerge from the pool to take off our old clothes and put on a new suit of clothes) – all these results of grace are beautifully and perfectly portrayed in immersion.

So let no one say that immersion is only one of two or three possible methods of baptism. It is the only method mandated by Christ and taught by his apostles as sufficient to demonstrate visibly the full glory of God's grace in our salvation. We do a serious injustice to men and women and to the gospel to offer them a choice between sprinkling, affusion and immersion, as if we had such a choice and that whatever method we chose, made little difference. We are diminishing the power of the 'visible word' of baptism and placing those believers who are baptized by sprinkling or affusion in the unenviable situation of doubting the validity of their baptism and of choosing whether or not to be immersed.

We do not allow believers the luxury of such a choice in the Lord's Supper! As evangelicals who seek to take God's Word seriously, we do not suggest that the communicants can either eat and drink the elements or take them home and put them in a glass jar on the mantle-piece where they can look at them all week and remember Christ's death. No, eating the bread and drinking the wine symbolise our personal appropriation of the benefits of our Saviour's death for our sin. To tamper with a sign is to change or diminish its meaning, and we have no right whatever to take such a liberty however helpful or convenient we may deem it to be.

With those who are the casualties of this confusion which has unnecessarily been allowed to drag on and on, I truly sympathise. Yours is a painful decision to make if you have been baptized as a believer but not by immersion. In the end, you alone, through much prayer and study, must decide what to do. Baptists, Pentecostalists and many others believe that baptism is not valid without immersion, just as Holy Communion is invalid if the elements are not consumed by the participants.

I would add a further incentive. Churches will only reform their unbiblical practice of sprinkling as pressure is brought upon them to deal with the issue by those members who insist on being immersed. If everyone affected acquiesces in sprinkling, the confusion and agony of conscience will only continue. A protest has to be made if reformation is to continue.

(3) Improving our baptism

If baptism is a sacrament signifying God's grace giving salvation and our faith grasping it, the rite should be a continuing influence for good in our lives. Though it is never to be repeated, it is ever to be remembered. Thus the Reformers often spoke of 'making use of' and 'improving' our baptism, by which they meant making use of its promises to strengthen our faith, hope, love, joy and obedience.

This is certainly Paul's purpose in Romans 6. To those who would justify continued sin in a Christian's life, he says in effect, 'Think again about your baptism. First, it was a kind of *funeral* service in which you celebrated your death with Christ to the old life of sin and your resurrection with him to a new life of holiness. How, then, can you who died to sin still live in it?' That's Paul's argument. Baptism rightly understood and remembered helps us to reckon ourselves 'to be dead indeed to sin, but alive to God in Christ Jesus our Lord' (Rom. 6:11).

Secondly, we should also look back on our baptism as a *marriage* service in which we were betrothed to Christ (2 Cor. 11:2). 'Baptism reminds me whose I am and whom I serve; who it is that stands pledge to love and cherish me, and share with me eternally all that he has, and what love and loyalty I owe in return' (J. Packer).

Thirdly, our baptism was a ceremony of *washing* in which the once-for-allness of baptism assures us of the once-for-allness of justification. The 'blood of Jesus Christ his Son cleanses us from all sin' (past, present and future, 1 John 1:7). And we can sing:

Jesus, thy blood and righteousness
My beauty are, my glorious dress;
Midst flaming worlds, in these arrayed,
With joy shall I lift up my head.

Bold shall I stand in that great day,
For who aught to my charge shall lay?
Fully absolved through these I am,
From sin and fear, from guilt and shame.

Count Zinzendorf, translated by John Wesley

Fourthly, as an act of *initiation* into the membership of the visible church, our baptism reminds us that we are not alone. We belong to God's wonderful family where we are as committed to each other as we are to him. We are part of a fellowship where we can find mutual help and support, and where we are committed to a life of worship, witness and work for our Father's glory.

Fifthly, as a service of *anticipation*, our baptism proclaims not only the resurrection of our spirit with Christ now, but also our body at the end of this age. Pre-eminently backward looking, it is not exclusively so. Like the sacrament of the Lord's Supper, it is also forward-looking, as Paul avers 'Buried with Him in baptism, in which you also were raised with Him through faith in the working of God, who raised Him from the dead (Col. 2:12). Baptism, in which we are claimed by Christ, points us forward to the resurrection of our bodies: 'Knowing that He who raised up the Lord Jesus will also raise us up with Jesus, and will present us with you' (2 Cor. 2:14). It helps us to lay hold with firmer grasp the promise of Jesus, 'This is the will of

Him who sent me, that everyone who sees the Son and believes in Him may have everlasting life; and I will raise Him up at the last day' (John 6:40). Contemplating our baptism, we, like Paul, can be 'sure that He who began a good work in (us) will bring it to completion at the day of Jesus Christ'.

This is how you and I can improve our baptism. Not by repeating it, but by regularly recalling the event so that we might enter into its reality afresh and renew our faith, hope, love, joy and obedience to Christ. Baptism is a once-for-all experience. Discovering its significance takes a lifetime!

(4) Some difficult situations

We live in a complex world where many people find themselves in difficult situations regarding baptism. To those baptized as infants (whether by immersion or sprinkling) and are then converted at a later age, I believe it is their duty to be properly baptized by immersion upon profession of their faith in Christ crucified and risen. This has been dealt with under the second heading part 1, especially paragraph six.

To those baptized by immersion upon profession of faith, and who then later realise they were not then converted, I believe that it would be wrong for them to ask to be re-baptized. The reasons why I say this are given under heading two part one, especially paragraph three.

To those baptized as believers by sprinkling or affusion, I believe they need to seek guidance from the Holy Spirit by much prayer and study of God's Word. My personal conviction is that the mode of baptism is very important. This is not just a difference in the amount of water used, but a difference in the picture which the visible word portrays. When you discard immersion, the picture to all intents and purposes has gone! If we are going to obey the Lord's command, we must comply with it fully. See point 2 part two, especially paragraphs four and five.

To those baptized as believers by immersion, but who have never been accepted into the membership of any church, I believe that their baptism is valid and that they should be accepted into the membership of the church they wish to join on the basis of a letter affirming their baptism by the church or group of persons who baptized them. Failing such a letter, their word should then be taken as sufficient.

----

[1] There is an interesting note on this issue in *The Life and Works of Joseph Kinghorn*, Vol. 1, p.450 (reprinted by the Particular Baptist Press, Springfield, Missouri, USA, 1995). Kinghorn, the well known pastor of St Mary's Baptist Church in Norwich, England, from 1790 to his death in 1832, was consulted on the issue of rebaptism. His position is exactly the one I hold.

'A singular case occurred in one of these churches in the year 1821: a person offered himself for membership, but at the same time disclosed the fact that he had been previously baptized, and joined a Baptist church, but had fallen into a sinful course, and remained in that state many years. He now professed to have received spiritual life, which he had never previously known experimentally, and the question arose, was his baptism a scriptural one or not? Reference was made to Rev. William Jones, of London, and to Mr Kinghorn. Mr Jones was of the opinion that such baptism was not scriptural, as it was administered to one who had not at the time received the grace of God, and that, he should be rebaptized. Mr Kinghorn, on the contrary, maintained that as the person had been immersed on a profession of his faith, all had been done that was required by the Saviour, as it was always impossible to ascertain with certainty the reality of such profession. The person in question was ultimately admitted to membership without being baptized again.'